C000201144

My time in the Special Forces was often spent [...] tom of a pint glass wishing the madness wou[...] on the 'reality check' rollercoaster and when [...] left with a solid plan of how to beat alcohol a[...] sion of you. Do yourself a favour, read the boc[...]

JAMES MENDAY SAS VETERAN AND FORMER CHELSEA FOOTBALL CLUB BODYGUARD

I enjoyed the book, amazing stuff. Alcohol is a horrendous drug, it nearly killed me countless times. But no matter your situation, you can transform your life. I highly recommend you give it a read. Thanks mate.

RHYS THOMAS, FORMER INTERNATIONAL RUGBY PLAYER

This is f*$king brilliant! I love the way you roll. This is really going to help people who perhaps have an issue or are maybe drinking a bit too much. I love the way you lay it out in a non-patronising way. 10 out of 10. Absolute genius.

AARON PHIPPS, PARALYMPIC GOLD MEDALIST

This book has turned me into an alcohol-free beer connoisseur.

STEVEN GREEN, FORMER EDITOR "THE OXFORD DRINKER"

Real Men Quit is superbly written. Hilarious and poignant, it had me glued to every page. It's one of those books you would gladly recommend to your friends and then march them down to the bookstore to ensure they bought it.

DANIEL DZIKOWSKI, EMOTIONAL WELLBEING SPEAKER AND COACH

Real Men Quit is exactly how you should approach life, understanding that it's serious but that you can have fun too. Duncan is a master at breaking truths down to be approachable through humour and understandable actions that can be taken! If you are unsure what change you want to make in life, this book is a great place to start!

RJ ZIMMERMAN, FOUNDER OF THE UNTAPPED KEG

Real Men Quit is like having a peek inside the mind of a very strange person, and then realising it's your own mind. Duncan systematically dismantles all the reasons for relying on alcohol while making you feel like you're having a chat with a mate down the... well, pub I suppose. The impact of Real Men Quit sneaks in under the radar, as you guffaw.

GEORGE ANDERSON, PERFORMANCE EXPERT AND ELITE
FITNESS RACER

Duncan is real, he quit and his life is beyond anything he ever thought it could be. He'll take you through the steps so you can overcome alcohol, He'll simplify the complex struggle towards the life you deserve. He's also a closet comedian. Real Men Quit is a belly laughin', mind blowin', life changin' read.

GETHIN JONES, PRISON REFORMER AND AUTHOR

Real Men Quit will help you even if you think you have zero willpower and slightly less determination. It will show you how to change. It will challenge you to stop making excuses. Duncan presents a simple and effective way to sort out your drinking without white knuckles. Grab a copy and give it a go.

DR ANDREW J PICKERING, UNIVERSITY OF NOTRE DAME

Real Men Quit

A catalogue record for this book is available from the British Library

The moral right of the author has been asserted, including his right to party.

Cover design by Tanja Prokop

Back cover photograph by Martin Wackenier.

Interior design by Graciela Aničić

Illustrations by Iulian Thomas

ISBN: 978-1-9999665-3-9 (paperback)

ISBN: 978-1-9999665-4-6 (ebook)

ISBN: 978-1-9999665-5-3 (audiobook)

First Edition: December 2023

10 9 8 7 6 5 4 3 2 1

REAL MEN

QUIT

Duncan Bhaskaran Brown

Medical warning

This book is not intended as a substitute for medical advice. Should you experience any medical problems visit a doctor and if the symptoms become severe seek urgent medical assistance. Don't be a dumbass.

In memory of Jon.
In praise of those who offered him love.

CONTENTS PAGE

SECTION

A Crack in Everything

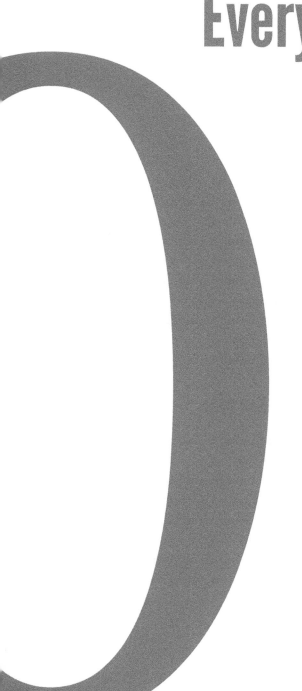

Sitting opposite me was one of the strongest people I'd ever met. He was durable, disciplined and daunting.

He'd completed the Royal Marine Commando training. You might not know that this is the longest infantry training programme in the world. But you *know* it requires willpower, strength and what the Americans call intestinal fortitude. Weak people don't get into the Marines. But the Marines was not enough; he went on to pass selection and serve for six years in the Special Boat Service. Now that requires elite levels of determination.

He's what's known in the trade as one of the tough kids.

Man down

Yet since leaving the forces his drinking had increased with the pressures of running his own business.

You wouldn't think that someone who had the dedication to join the cream of the British Armed Forces would have any problem stopping drinking. After all, rock-solid self-control should be enough.

Despite the fact that he had everything else in his life squared away, he was struggling to manage his drinking. For some people that wouldn't make sense but for me it wasn't even surprising.

You cannot use guts to control drinking.

If someone as strong as him can be made weak by alcohol then we all can. No shame. If someone as mentally tough as him can get caught in the trap of alcohol then we all can. No stigma. If someone as robust as him can get overwhelmed by alcohol then we all can. No judgement here brother.

That don't make no sense

He told me that he was confused by his drinking. He couldn't understand it – when he finished work he'd drop into his chair and think "god I'm stressed, I need a drink", and when he was on holiday he'd drop into his deckchair and think, "god I'm relaxed, I need a drink". Why was that?

When he was working he needed to drink because he was stressed. But when he was on holiday he needed to drink because he wasn't stressed. How did that work? In the dusty bit at the back of his brain, the bit he'd try not to visit too often, he knew that it just didn't add up.

I asked him if he'd heard of Leonard Cohen.

He shook his head.

Even though I knew he wasn't going to get my reference I smiled. He had the crack. The good news is that to get control of your drinking you don't require an elite level of mental toughness. You need the crack.

What a Guy

You're smart. And I can prove it. Only smart men buy this book. You're creative. Of course you are – you took one look at the cover and said "Nice design work, Duncan". I like you already.

And you're strong. Not because you can pick up the sheer weight of profundity that is *Real Men Quit*. No, you're strong because you're a drinker. And all drinkers are strong. In my experience we're also smart and creative.

That said, we're usually a little south of perfect.

I hope you're not all worked out and completely wrapped up, because this book is not for flawless men. If this book is going to have any effect, you need a fault line. Do you have the crack?

More importantly, are you familiar with Leonard Cohen's back catalogue? He sang "There is a crack, a crack in everything. That's how the light gets in."

My guess is that you need the light, so let's hope you have a crack somewhere other than the back of your pants.

Does that sound familiar?

All you need at the moment is a dim, half-formed thought that maybe, just maybe, the way you see alcohol might, perhaps, possibly, mayhap, feasibly be a bit wrong. That's the crack; the chip in the pint glass, the fissure in the wine bottle, the rent in the barrel of twenty-four-year-old single malt whisky that for some reason tastes like TCP.

If you have that tinge of suspicion then hello my friend, you're in the right place. That's the crack.

 Hallelujah brother, get ready for the light.

If you think that alcohol is perfect, that it's the nectar of the gods and that only a fool would limit himself, then you'll still enjoy this book. There are jokes.

The three bullet-holes of change

I want to be completely honest with you. Throughout this book I want you to know exactly what I'm doing. This isn't a miracle cure: you don't have to bow your head while I lay my hands on you and you get saved by the power of my ego. That would be just plain weird.

I want you to understand what we're doing. Because if you do then you won't just go beyond booze, you'll travel all the way to the life you've dreamed of. Oh yes, even *those* things!

Here's the plan. Grab your semi-automatic, twelve-bore behaviour-change gun and let's get shooting. Don't panic, you don't have to shoot like my SBS buddy – this isn't special forces sniper school. This is late night, redneck, shooting at rusty street signs. Accuracy ain't important, just squeeze off a shot.

We're going to create the three bullet-holes of change. They're called that because I thought the graphic would look cool.

As you can see, I wasn't wrong.

Three is the magic number

And yes, there will be lots of armchair machismo. In fact, this book is filled with touchline toughness like the average bodybuilder is pumped full of steroids. There will also be three sections.

CHALLENGE YOUR ASSUMPTIONS

The first section will help you to look at the things you believe about alcohol. I'm going to point out some stuff and ask the odd question but I'm not going to tell you what to believe. You're a big boy; you're perfectly capable of forming your own attitudes and values.

CHANGE YOUR THOUGHTS

The next section will look at your thoughts. Not in a weird 1950s CIA mind control way – we'll just examine your thought process. This might mean you decide to alter the way you think. But, again, I'm not going to come round your house and strap you to a chair, I really don't work for the CIA. Honestly, I was just pretending to be a spy. To impress a girl. Didn't work.

CHOOSE NEW ACTIONS

The final section is about how you act. Not so much the drinking – we are going to look at your whole life. If that sounds a bit scary, be cool. There are many pages between here and there, boobs will be mentioned frequently and there will be more than one nob gag. You also have permission to fart.

Look, it's really important for me to clear this up now, I don't force people to do things. I can categorically state that I have never attached electrodes to anyone's genitals, except my own. And that wasn't nearly as much fun as I was hoping.

Over the coming pages you're going to learn three things about me.
- I have a questionable sense of humour.
- My references, like Bessie Bonehill's, are obscure.
- I like to celebrate.

So let's party. In fact, tonight I'm gonna party like it's 1999.

" Me, I'd like to think life is like a drink and I'm hoping that it tastes like bourbon.

THE WONDER STUFF

It's not that I need Jon to have fun, but where he went the good times followed. And today I needed good times.

My rapidly-warming lager was sprinting to the bottom of the glass. The bar was packed tight with blokes whose arms were like oak and whose brains were like lumber. They were all trying to outshout the jukebox and, in the spirit of petty reprisal, the barman kept cranking up the volume.

And still there was no Jon.

"Let's have another one," Hank shouted. It was barely audible. Not surprising, Hank was titchy, a scrawny lad among a forest of men.

"Good plan, chap!" I reply with a forced grin. I turned to the bar but my route was blocked by a broad back – was that bark under his shirt? There was no path, there was no way to the promised land. I was stuck in between – want a drink, can't get a drink.

I felt like I was shrinking. Which was problematic because my clothes remained the same size. I was about to disappear into my humorously embossed t-shirt.

"I'm getting thirsty here," Hank shouted.

Thirsty? I was drowning in my own clothing. There was only insecurity. The scene was shot over with a patina of doubt, a thin film of ambiguity, an unvocalised disquiet. And my trousers were about to fall down.

Seconds before I was debagged, there was a subtle vibration in the molecular structure of the pub's atmosphere. The volume of the music dropped, the crowd repelled like opposing magnets, the doors swung open unaided, as if some ineffable force was clearing the way.

Suddenly Jon.

Reliably late. Stressfully relaxed. Ethereally down to earth. Just Jon.

"I'd have been here earlier but..." he said as he filled a hole that didn't appear to be there. "...there was this blonde and..." He trailed off as he noticed my empty glass. "You do know that they sell beer here?"

"Well, I..." as I responded his gaze shifted. He surveyed the bar like a lion glancing casually across the savannah.

"Same again." It wasn't a question.

He drifted into a non-existent space at the bar. He nudged aside a giant redwood in a cheap, checked shirt – if I'd done that I'd have got beaten to a pulp.

In less time than it took me to find somewhere to put my empty glass he was back, managing to levitate pints and chasers without spilling a drop.

"Shorts?" I ask, looking at the booze.

"Vodka corrupts," he smiled. "And Absolut Vodka corrupts absolutely." He drained the diminutive glass with aplomb. "It's good to be home."

"You call this home?" I asked as I raised the liquor.

"Yes Duncan, this is our spiritual home, the Mecca of our merrymaking."

"I don't think they have pubs in Mecca."

"Stop thinking, stop being a part time hedonist. Commit, damn you."

"I'd like to..."

"Stop liking, start living. No more Mr Nice Chops – nice is bland. We're young, gifted and drunk!"

He paused, his face broad with grin.

"I've got to work…" I began.

"Work? Smirk! Do you have beer?" he replied like he was felling a tree.

"Well… yeah."

"Do you have friends?" Another swing of the axe.

"Yeah!"

"Do you have a place to stand?" Thwack.

"Yeah?"

"So let's drink the world." Timber.

I could do this. I could drown the doubt. This evening was going to be epic. The day after? I curse thee tomorrow. I could drink my way through this.

The raucous evening was just beginning, I was going to make sure it never ended. I threw the vodka throatward.

"Eureka!" I cheered like I'd just discovered a fundamental principle of fluid dynamics.

"And if our luck holds we shall run naked through the streets of Syracuse tonight." Jon's face erupted in Cheshire glee.

SECTION

1

Challenge your assumptions

DRINKING IS FUN

I was a shy kid but I found an outlet at Scouts. I loved the outdoors, I was never happier than when I was camping or pioneering or getting muddy on an assault course. But then things started to move on. My limited group of friends stopped being interested in badges and started becoming interested in girls.

This was a problem. I was uncomfortable in social situations and petrified of women. There was this ravenous force inside me that was desperate to get closer to the opposite sex, yet there was another part of me that was scared stiff of even uttering one syllable to them. There was an immovable obstacle in front of my unstoppable desire.

Then I discovered alcohol. I thought all my Christmases had come at once. It seemed to offer so much. It helped me to socialise, it brought me friends, it cured my shyness, it eased my stress. Best of all, most beautiful of all, it impressed the girls. It allowed me to be funny and cool and confident and it even compensated for my teenage fear of showering. Well, mostly. It was so effective I ended up with a girlfriend.

 Alcohol solved all my problems. I was all in from the start.

My late teens and early twenties played out like an advert. I was strong, sexy, fun: the nights out were legendary, the bonds of friendship unbreakable and the women, oh the women! Life couldn't get any better and it was all down to alcohol.

Believing the hype

Or so I thought. And it was understandable that I thought that way. True, we're talking about the days before memes and Netflix but the world was still awash with witty and intelligent messages about alcohol and how great it was. I got them from the TV, and magazines, from my musical idols and my sporting heroes but most of all I got them from my friends. Heck, I even got them from my parents.

You know what I'm talking about because, unless you happened to grow up in an off-grid commune, your childhood was in the same environment of booze-soaked messaging.

Given that you've picked up this book you've probably started to wonder how true all those messages were. You're probably starting to question whether alcohol helps you with your stress, whether it helps you have fun, whether it makes you strong. And horror of horrors, maybe it doesn't even make you look sexy.

Maybe you've even started to question whether you were only ever intelligent, good looking and funny because you're basically intelligent, good looking and funny and in fact alcohol just made you look like a par-boiled idiot with a lopsided smile and subprime sense of humour.

That's cool. You have the crack. You want the light. You're among friends. You're sophisticated enough to know that there's more to the truth than the adverts would have you believe. You have enough street-smarts to question the powers that be.

And that's all you need to do. You just need to question what you've been told about alcohol. Nothing more. So long as you're open to the possibility that you may have been sold a half-truth then you'll be OK. That's what you need to focus on at the moment. Don't change anything about your life right away. In fact, you don't even have to stop drinking.

DRINKING IS FUN

Don't stop?

Yes, you read that correctly, you don't need to stop drinking. You can continue to drink alcohol while you're reading this book. By which I mean you can drink alcohol as you usually would rather than you should read this book drunk.

Never drink and read, it's hard. Trust me, I've tried struggling through the mental fog and reading with one eye shut so that I could focus on the words. That exam didn't go well.

What I'm saying is don't worry about drinking now. Drink as normal. There will be plenty of time to think about not drinking later; for now we're just going to challenge your assumptions about alcohol. If you try to stop drinking now you'll probably fail because there's a lot you need to figure out before you can stop successfully.

Try not to change anything else about your life. Don't start training for an ultramarathon, that would be stressful. Don't start trading crypto, that would be an unnecessary drain on your mental resources. Don't decide that now is the dead centre of your life and what this crisis requires is a motorbike. Dealing with alcohol is enough. It is your number one problem so focus on that.

Let me be super clear: I'm saying you shouldn't add stress to your life. I'm *not* saying poor you, life is so hard, you're not in the "right place" to quit, better put the book down and have a beer to commiserate.

There will never be a "right place" or a "right time" or a "right life". There will always be stress, there will always be things that'll give you the excuse not to bother.

Don't sweat the stuff you can't control. Don't decide that now is the time for an extensive overhaul of your garage. Don't procrastinate.

It's time to reaffirm your status as a real man. It's time to quit.

Arghhhhhhhhh!

You just read the word quit. I'm aware that this word may fill you full of fear. But that's OK. Fear is normal. It doesn't mean you are weak; it doesn't mean you're not a real man, it doesn't mean that you're a scrawny weakling who is destined to be picked on by the bigger boys. No, it simply means you have fear.

How does it feel?

I don't want to give you the idea that this is a book about emotions. I guarantee you that it will not feature primal scream therapy or laughter yoga. But the way you feel about any change is important.

I've helped a lot of men stop doing a lot of stupid things over the years and what I've noticed is that they tend to be slightly anxious or worried at this point. And that's cool. You're contemplating something big. Something that you probably aren't sure you can manage. Something that you might not even think is possible.

You have a ton of head-junk around alcohol. You probably believe that you won't enjoy social situations without alcohol. You probably believe that you need alcohol to deal with stress. You probably believe that you won't be as funny, creative, rebellious and rock'n'roll without alcohol. You're worried that without alcohol you won't be you and your life will suck. If I say that I'm going to take your drink away it's likely to cause a sandstorm of fear.

Don't worry, that's completely normal.

 Don't fear the fear, in the fear is excitement.

Let's face it, you wouldn't be reading a book like this if there wasn't a part of you that wanted to change. You wouldn't even have got this far if you couldn't see the possibility of a new way of living – an exciting, shiny, fresh way of living. There's a little bit of excitement too. Probably more fear than excitement, but that's cool. 90% fear and 10% excitement is normal.

Fear/Excitement – Excitement/Fear

Interestingly, when your brain feels *fear* it triggers a physical reaction: your breathing and your heart rate go up, your palms get sweaty and your pupils dilate. When your brain experiences *excitement* it triggers a physical reaction: your breathing and your heart rate go up, your palms get sweaty and your pupils dilate.

Yes, fear and excitement are basically the same thing. Over the next few chapters, we're going to work on reinterpreting that fear as excitement. The good news is that you're really good at that – or at least your brain is.

Have you ever bungee-jumped? Skied? Forgotten her birthday? Anything that's dangerous makes you a little bit scared; don't worry, it happens to the best of us. Yet, once you've finished, your brain doesn't remember fear, it remembers elation. Clever, hey?

 Your brain remembers fear as excitement.

What's even smarter is that research from Harvard Business School by Professor A.W. Brooks has found you can change the feeling before the event. So if you're feeling fearful, shout "I am excited!". True, people will think you're weird if you do it at the quarterly sales meeting.

Fear or excitement? It's just a matter of how you look at it.

Great, but am I going to have to quit?

Look, I'm not going to force you to do anything. My operational philosophy doesn't include waterboarding.

And anyway, you're a grown-ass man, you make your own decisions. When the time comes you can make up your own mind. You can decide what the right path for you is. Maybe it's stopping, maybe it's moderation, maybe it's unabashed hedonism. Whatever it is, when the time comes it'll be your choice. For now, just don't worry about it.

I'm going to offer you some ideas that might challenge your assumptions. And maybe that'll change your thinking. And then maybe you'll choose some new actions. Whatever happens, you make up your own mind.

ONE SIMPLE INSTRUCTION

'm only going to ask you to do one thing (apart from the fact that I've already asked you to think about alcohol, not stop drinking and not add unnecessary stress). OK, I'm only going to ask you to do one *more* thing, because I'm so demanding.

I want you to say the words "Real Men Quit" when you make a cup of coffee every morning. Simple.

So simple I'm now going to spend an entire chapter patronising you about how to do it.

Wake up and smell the beverage

I want you to think about the first cup of coffee of the day. If you don't drink coffee, think about the first drink of the day. You're smart enough to substitute the word coffee with cold filtered yak's milk if that's your refreshment.

If you're anything like most blokes you have that coffee at the same time every day. Where are you? What time is it? What are you wearing? Picture the scene. Got it?

Great, now think about it. Do you boil a kettle? Do you use a stove-top? Do you fire up a machine? Order it from your local hipster barista? Imagine the details, in particular the sound and smell.

I want you to pick a very precise moment, like when you push the button on the coffee machine or when you open the fridge door.

Every morning when that very specific moment happens, when you see it, hear it and smell it I want you to say, "Real Men Quit". You don't have to say it out loud, you can just say it in your head. If you fancy chanting it like some sort of virile, sober soldier then don't let me stand in your way.

Once you've said the words – smile. Anything from a subtle curling of the lips to a maniacal grin. Celebrate. Celebrate the fact that you remembered to do it. Celebrate the fact that you've started the day well. Celebrate the fact that you've taken a step on an important journey. True, it's only one step but a journey of a thousand steps starts with a single cliche.

The sight, sound and smell of the coffee is a trigger to remind you to complete the action. Saying "Real Men Quit" to yourself is the action and smiling afterwards is a way of celebrating the action. Trigger, Action, Celebration. That's the heart of the Tactical Change System. I'm sure you'll agree it has a hardcore, militaristic vibe. We're going to go way deeper into the Tactical Change System in a bit.

Duncan, I don't like coffee

Alright, you don't drink coffee. That's OK. Hang it on what you do drink. Hear the sound of the OJ pouring into the glass, the tea bag squeezed into the mug, or the gentle lowing of the yak as you tug its udders.

Whatever you're drinking there will be a sight, a sound and, if we're talking yak, a smell associated with it. Conjure up that scene and connect it with the words "Real Men Quit".

Trigger, Action, Celebration. Tactical. Lock and load, soldier.

And if all else fails put a sticky note on the kettle.

Do it every day. Maybe you think it's pointless, maybe you think I'm odd. Or maybe you can see where I'm going with this. Let's just say that this is a change – a very small change and, if nothing else, it will help you see that you're capable of making changes.

To recap, the one thing that I want you to do is:
- Question what you've been told about alcohol.
- Keep an open mind.
- Change as little as possible in your life.
- Definitely don't stop drinking.
- Say "Real Men Quit" when you make your first coffee of the day.
- Oh, and read the rest of the book.

Not a lot.

" Street's like a jungle. So call the police

ALBARN, COXON, JAMES & ROWNTREE.

Flashes. Flashes of sound. Drums. Guitars. Hammond organ? Flash of lights. Probably a club, could be an ambulance. Flashes of sweat. Writhing bodies too close to be strangers. Flashes of fear. Where's my drink?

"Confidence is a preference for the habitual voyeur of what is known as..." Phil Daniels speak-sings in a sanguine lilt.

"Parklife!" we shout back like raucous acolytes.

But what really flashed in the pan was a face. Just a flash. A brief snatch of a breath-taker, heartbreaker, booty shaker. A dark-skinned angel. Lakshmi's little sister, less arms, more attitude.

I wanted to fall at her feet and worship but there was a lot of beer on the floor. And she'd probably think that I'd just passed out. Maybe I had passed out? Maybe she was just a dream?

"We're going outside for a smoke," Jon bellowed into my ear.

"Cool."

I look back across the dripping machinery of party.

And just like that, the dream was gone.

REAL MEN DRINK

Imagine you're in a pub. You've just bought a round – you're generous like that. As you're walking back to your table full of great mates you overhear a snatch of conversation.

"Finish your beer, you big girl's blouse."

Do you think about it? Does it even register?

Probably not. But maybe it should make you think. Maybe you should stop and spend a moment considering it. I mean, is drinking beer slowly really a sign of weakness? What's the assumption that lies beneath that statement? Drinking is a sign of strength, a sign of masculinity. But do real men drink?

Belief disposal

Your actions are underpinned by your beliefs. Why do you vote? You believe it's important. Why do you read? You believe it relaxes you or it might teach you something. Why do you listen to Oasis? You believe music stopped in the mid-nineties. Beliefs matter.

To get to grips with your drinking you need to get to grips with the beliefs that underlie it. To do that, we're going to go through a process.

What we're going to do is make the subconscious conscious, using what I like to call the Belief Disposal System.

I like to call it that because it sounds a bit like bomb disposal and I like to make things sound unnecessarily militaristic. Basically, I haven't gotten over the fact that my parents never bought me the Action Man helicopter. And they're like £200 on eBay now – boy do I need to sell a few more copies of this book.

IDENTIFY

Start by identifying your beliefs. Bring them into the light. That's the first step of making the unconscious process that drives your behaviour conscious. You can't work on what you can't see.

EXAMINE

Once you can see them, you need to assess them honestly. Are they true or are they just things you believe? Crucially, do they serve you? Are these beliefs getting you closer to being the man you want to be?

EXPLODE

Decide whether to keep the belief or not. If it's no longer helpful then pack it full of Semtex and blow it smithereens. Fire in the hole.

The name's Booze

Let's dive in headfirst, let's start with brute manliness. Who's the most manly man that you can think of?

Yes, that's right, James Bond. He's strong, he's confident, he gets the job done and, best of all, after he's finished he goes home with the sexiest woman in the film.

And he drinks. You know what he drinks, you know how he likes it mixed and you probably have opinions as to whether or not that's the right way to make the drink. God, do you know that James Bond likes a beverage.

When Ian Fleming thought up the character, he didn't say to himself, "I'm going to create an advert for booze". Part of him subconsciously created an advert for a glamorous lifestyle and it involved a lot of alcohol mixed in with the trembling women, thudding bullets and throbbing cars. But he wasn't paid by the alcohol industry.

However, the franchise is now. True, it's advertised many things – from watches to cars, credit cards to airlines, running shoes to razors. It also single-handedly ensured Walther remains a viable firearms manufacturer.

But you don't have a problem with watches or razors and I'm guessing you don't even own a PPK, so let's look at booze. Bond has advertised the lot: Bollinger, Heineken, Macallan, Château Angélus, Smirnoff, even that staple of the British Secret Service, Jack Daniels.

You can't doubt that the makers of the movies have been trying to get you to associate James Bond with booze for years. And it's worked.

If you can recognise that James Bond, and all the other films and TV shows, have helped you to believe that alcohol makes you strong, sophisticated, great with women and handy with a firearm then you've taken the first step.

The next step is asking if it's true.

Think about Daniel Craig in his swimming trunks – bear with me for a second – in that famous scene on the beach in Casino Royale. How much do you think alcohol had to do with that six pack?

Boozy Galore

Granted, Daniel Craig drinks. I'm not denying that – in fact he famously got drunk on vodka

Martinis the day he found out he'd got the part. But in the preparation of that scene how much did alcohol play a part?

In *Intelligent Fitness*, Daniel Craig's personal trainer talks extensively about his regime before and during the shooting of the Bond films. Funnily enough he didn't mention alcohol. He mentioned a lot of weights, cardio and stretching. He mentioned a lot of 5am starts. He mentioned a lot of gut-wrenching, will-sapping plyometric exercises that I hope I never have to do. But not once did he suggest to Daniel Craig that he should drink alcohol as part of his fitness regime. Espresso yes, Martini no.

Now you might think I'm taking this point a little far, but I want to be clear on this: the image you have of Bond isn't built with alcohol. It's used to sell alcohol but no alcohol was involved in the creation of the image. In fact, Daniel Craig drank way less when he was playing Bond than he would normally.

The image is Bond = alcohol. The reality is Bond = no alcohol.

For now, all you need to do is realise that there's a difference between the image and the reality. There's a mismatch between the claims they make about the product and what it actually does.

By putting a Martini into James Bond's hand, they're hoping that the strength, the sophistication, the power and the raw man energy will rub off on the drink, despite the fact that the bloke playing Bond is drinking far less than he normally would while he's creating the image.

 If you can see that there is an illusion, then you've taken an important step.

REAL MEN CHOOSE

When was the last time you went to a celebration that didn't involve alcohol? Not in recent memory, probably not in your adult life. Because even if we do something that requires sobriety, like go karting or kitesurfing, we get drunk afterwards.

You've got to wonder why that is.

Why are fun and alcohol so intrinsically linked? Why is birth, death and everything in between celebrated with beer or, better yet, champagne? Is booze really some Jovian bringer of jollity?

Many of our ideas about alcohol come from advertising. A huge amount of the imagery used in alcohol adverts depicts young, good looking people having fun. It's all well dressed, bright eyed, sex bunnies having social media perfect nights out even before the socials were a thing.

But let's think about that for a second. Do your nights out live up to the images presented?

There's a particular Jose Cuervo ad that always sticks in my mind. The strap line is "I bust loose with my buddies and Cuervo". What strikes me is how drop dead gorgeous all his buddies are. He clearly has no male friends – his friendship circle is half a dozen smokin' hot sex ornaments. It's clear that he'll be sleeping with at least one of them in the next ten minutes and all of them if he has the energy.

Maybe that's you. Maybe that's your life. Maybe you should be visiting the doctor to get some cream to sooth your poor over-worked manstick.

But maybe it's not. Maybe that doesn't exactly describe the relationship that you have with booze. Maybe that's not a representative example of the kind of social events you attend.

Which begs the question: why do you believe that alcohol helps you to socialise? Is there another mismatch?

Russian Choice

Let's think about it from another direction. I'm going to assume you aren't a fan of the works of Vladimir Putin. If you are, wow, how's that working out for you?

Let's assume you've figured out that he became a psychopath after being bullied because his head looks like a turnip. Therefore, you've got to wonder why he's so popular in Russia.

I mean it can't be the secret police. There's about 150 million Russians – you'd need a lot of coppers to keep them in line. No, there's more to it than that. A significant number of people in Russia must believe that turnip head is a good option as President.

Seriously? How did he pull that one?

The answer is simpler than you'd think. The people of Russia believe they have the best president in the history of democracy because that's all they've ever been told. All of the TV stations and print media in Russia are either controlled by the state, tow the line or have given up.

You might be thinking that this isn't a problem because the truth is on Facebook. Except you can't get Facebook, Twitter or Instagram in Russia. True, there's VK, the Russian government owned social media platform. Or you could bypass the big wall Russia has put around the internet but the sentence for sharing Putin's definition of fake news is 15 years in Siberia.

What the vast majority of Russians hear, the vast majority of the time, is a story about Europe and America sneakily keeping Russia weak, a story about Putin being a fantastic, tough guy, bravely standing up for his country and not having a root vegetable noggin. A story that would have you believe that invading Ukraine is a totally legitimate way to regain territory that was stolen from the motherland.

I know that sounds ridiculous, but only because you don't hear it all the time. If it was all you ever heard on TV, all your friends talked about, all you saw online, then you'd probably believe it too.

You can see that total immersion in Putin's grand story makes people believe stuff that you think is rubbish.

You can probably also see that if things are going to change then the first thing the Russian population needs to do is to challenge their assumptions.

Challenge alcohol

How does that relate to alcohol? Would it be fair to say that many times you've heard people say how great alcohol is? Would be it fair to say that you've seen people enjoying alcohol on TV? Would it be fair to say that you've heard a lot about how great alcohol is online?

True, no one is going to send you to the gulag if you disagree but you have to admit that support for the positive benefits of alcohol is pretty widespread.

Everywhere you turn someone is there to tell you that alcohol cures stress, helps you relax, improves social situations, makes you strong and that hot sex is simply a few beers away.

But there's one crucial difference. You have a choice – not the choice Russian voters got, the choice of who comes a distant second – there's a real alternative. You don't have to choose what comes in miles behind alcohol, you can choose something other than drinking and being miserable.

Choose Tea

The other day I attended a networking event. Honestly, I don't like that sort of thing. Who does? While I knew that it was important and there'd be great opportunities, I was nervous.

I grabbed the lanyard with my name on and looked around the room. Sometimes you look at a group of people and it seems like they're all enjoying themselves and none of them want to talk to you. I got that impression, strongly. There was no one to talk to.

I went over to the refreshments and made a cup of tea, slowly. I used the time to size up the room and fairly soon I saw a conversation I could barge in on. I drank the tea and started to relax.

I doubt anyone would hear that story and say that tea relaxes you in social situations. No one would be expounding the benefits of tea as a social lubricant. No one would be thinking "I can only enjoy events if I've had several cups of tea."

If that story had involved alcohol, many people would have nodded sagely. "Yes," they'd say, "alcohol is amazing and it really helps in social situations".

Don't you think that's a bit strange?

Nerves are Natural

Being nervous in social situations is a natural human response. While walking into a room full of people you don't know isn't a life-or-death situation, that's how your brain sees it. Your brain is thinking if these people don't like me I'll be shunned and have to live outside the group, and that's a recipe for a gnarly death.

That's why it's natural to be nervous at the start of social events. It's also natural for those nerves not to last long. It's natural to relax into it. If you have a cup of tea you unwind a bit and you don't think about it, so why is it when we have a beer and feel calmer we say it was the beer that relaxed us?

That's a mismatch.

My daughter is seven so I find myself attending a lot of kids' parties. At the start the kids are often a bit shy. They hang around the edges and don't want to get involved. Give it five minutes and they're playing "who can tear the radiator off the wall first".

Are adults so different?

Kids don't need alcohol to enjoy social situations so why do we believe adults do? Is it because that's what we've been told? Could we be like the people of Russia? Could we believe things simply because we've heard them a lot?

" No alarms and no surprises, please.

GREENWOOD, O'BRIEN, GREENWOOD, SELWAY AND YORKE

I tried to get comfortable. There was nothing wrong with the sofa, the problem was my body. Whichever way I shuffled it felt like I was lying on concrete. Every nerve ending was set to a dull ache.

I had a faint hope that it was levelling out when a horrendous din jarred my fragile mind. It was coming from the kitchen. Like as not it was only Jon cooking but it sounded like a 183 tonne Acco Super Dozer fighting with Godzilla.

It forced me to my feet. I wandered into the kitchen expecting a wall to have come down. Frankly, structural collapse would have caused less damage. I'm not saying Jon was a messy cook but it looked like a hurricane had been through, followed by an earthquake and a spot of carpet bombing.

"Oh," I said.

"To create fried eggs you must first do some breaking," he replied in a voice that was far too chipper for the morning after.

"I get that you need to crack the eggs but was it necessary to smash the oven?"

"This will help," he handed me a cup of steaming coffee.

"I'm not sure I want coffee."

"You may not want it, but you need it." He smiled.

I looked at him sceptically.

"It'll make you feel better. Now drink up and despite your stunted musical acumen I'm going to trust you with the keys to the stereo."

I went over to the CD rack and started to browse. I was wondering if there was anything quiet when the Rolling Stones caught my eye. I took a swig of the coffee. It was thick, it was bitter, it was robust. But I kept it down. I guess Mick was right: you can't always get what you want. But if you try sometimes, well, you might find, you get what you need.

Jon slammed down two plates of fried goodness. Beauty is a relative thing, but these breakfasts could have graced the cover of Vogue.

"That is what you need," he said, spearing a sausage with his fork.

"I never got the difference between want and need. I feel like I need to have a threesome with both of the barmaids from The Midget."

"No," he said between bites, "you want to have a threesome, you need to figure out which one you have a better shot with."

I shoved a piece of bacon into my mouth. Salt. Fat. Relax.

"And don't worry about the tomato, I fried the nutrition out of it," he grinned.

45

REAL REAL MEN DRINK

J ames Bond is obviously not real; he's clearly an illusion. So let's have a look at some real men, and I mean real in every sense of the word.

Think about the sort of events that alcohol companies normally sponsor. You could argue that huge multinationals like Heineken, Molson Coors, C&C Group and Diageo spend enormous sums sponsoring rugby because they're trying to sell beer to men and it's men who watch rugby. But maybe they're also hoping that the strength, dedication and downright manliness of the players will rub off on their brands. And, let's be honest, it does.

But is it true? Having thought about Bond, are you starting to think that there may be a bit of an illusion here too? You see the strength and power of the sportsmen wearing the advertisers' logo and you connect the two. That's what they want you to think, but how much alcohol actually goes into the creation of those virtues?

I played rugby a bit when I was a lad. Partly for the socially acceptable violence, but mostly for the beer. Rugby players drink, and that's putting it mildly. But what about the pros? What about the guys that look like weightlifters, run like sprinters and throw like trebuchets? What about the Olympian gods of the egg-shaped ball?

Let's look at science. I asked my mate George Anderson – who looks like an Olympian god and happens to be a performance expert

– about alcohol and sport. He said, "It doesn't look good, Duncan." By that he meant that if you want to do some sport then drinking alcohol is a terrible idea.

The science bit

Sometimes I wonder about scientists. They did a study attempting to measure the effect of alcohol on endurance by giving people vodka while they ran on a treadmill. Many of the participants were unable to complete the exercise. Breaking news: vodka and treadmills don't mix.

Few sportsmen are stupid enough to play drunk – I mean, it's not the 70s. What about the effects of alcohol on recovery? Now, I'm about to quote a scientific paper and I don't want you to get the idea that this is going to happen a lot. This isn't an exercise physiology class. I won't do it again.

"Consumption of even moderate amounts of alcohol following eccentric based exercise [a fancy way of saying leg presses] magnifies the normally observed loss in dynamic and static strength."

The study, published in the Journal of Science and Medicine in Sport, shows that alcohol magnifies muscle pain and stuffs up your recovery.

 That post-game beer is making you weak.

And there are many other studies. Like the one that demonstrates that alcohol reduces work tolerance in cold temperatures. This would be a disadvantage if you play in the winter – rugby, I'm looking at you. Or another showing alcohol reduces the uptake and storage of muscle glycogen – that's less fuel for slamming into other big blokes. Or another on alcohol's role in increasing proinflammatory cytokines. My legs are hurting just reading all of this.

Look, I could go on – there are literally journals full of science-sounding words that all add up to the simple fact that "it doesn't look good, Duncan.".

That's the science. Alcohol impedes sporting performance. True, there are many complex mechanisms at play, but the bottom line is alcohol gets in the way of being an athlete. And in case you are tempted to say "oh well the science is always divided. You've picked the studies that support your argument." I haven't.

Research it if you want but you won't find any science that says alcohol improves sporting performance. The mechanism is straightforward: sport + alcohol = lower performance.

The elite of the elite

Some sportsmen drink, despite the fact that as little as an hour's research proves that it's dumb idea. But what about the best of the best? The ones that are so dedicated they can be bothered to google it?

How about Jonny Wilkinson? Maybe I'm living in the past, but he is the most recent Englishman to win World Rugby's Player of the Year, which often seems more like New Zealand's Player of the Year. And you must admit that he was a bit good. 1,179 points, 91 caps and one world cup win, not bad stats.

Jonny Wilkinson is teetotal. When he was playing he advertised plenty of alcohol, but he consumed none. He knew that elite sporting performance is incompatible with alcohol.

And he's not alone. Tom Brady doesn't drink. Novak Djokovic doesn't drink. Floyd Mayweather doesn't drink. Cristiano Ronaldo doesn't drink. And if you think that Ronaldo doesn't drink because he's too girly, neither does Harry Kane.

The point is that Jonny Wilkinson, winner of two Heineken Cups, does not drink. The booze giants use his skill, his dedication, his power, his tenacity, his strength and that funny wiggle thing to sell you booze. But all the time he's building those attributes without drinking a drop.

The image is rugby success = alcohol. The reality is the most successful player = no alcohol.

There's that mismatch again. There's the difference between the vehicle used to advertise the product and the features of the product. There's that illusion again.

No white coat required

I'm not going to argue that no sportsmen drink. I'm lucky to have several friends who have medals. One of them, who has a shiny gold one, said he had a relaxed attitude towards drinking. His idea of a relaxed attitude is probably puritanical compared to you; he didn't drink for a year before he won that big hunk of gold, though he might have had a little bit to drink afterwards.

But let's think for a moment about the sports people we associate with alcohol: George Best, Alex Higgins, Ricky Hatton and Paul Gascoigne. And how do we think about them? Wasted talent. Ruined lives.

Now let's review the list of people that don't drink. Jonny Wilkinson: greatest ever English rugby player. Tom Brady: most Superbowl wins. Novak Djokovic: most grand slams wins. Floyd Mayweather: 50 wins, zero losses. Cristiano Ronaldo: the single prettiest person ever to play any sport, ever. True sporting success, true strength, comes from either very limited drinking or no drinking.

Off the ball tackle?

Someone recently said to me, "yeah but what about Wayne Rooney? He drank and he was good". OK, compare him with Ronaldo. Rooney played top-flight football for 13 years. Ronaldo was smashing it into the onion bag for 19 years. That's a huge difference in longevity.

Given that there's clear evidence that alcohol has an impact on recovery, doesn't that six years difference show you that Rooney could have achieved so much more? England were shit when Rooney was captain, but now someone who doesn't drink is captain they're suddenly good. Coincidence?

Questions at the back of your mind

We've been sold this image of strong men drinking alcohol. All I'm asking you to do is question how true it is. Ask yourself, is Roger Federer holding that glass of champagne because champagne is an

integral part of his preparation routine or because he's a paid ambassador for Moet & Chandon?

Are the strong men that promote alcohol getting stronger because they drink alcohol? Or are they avoiding it? Aren't the ones that drink too much the ones that end up pissing their talent up the wall?

Look, I'm not asking you to agree that alcohol makes you weak. But can't you see that something isn't right? Can't you see that alcohol advertising doesn't add up. And if it's not true...

What else might not be true?

What other illusions might be floating around out there? What else might have snuck into your head? What other false beliefs about alcohol might you have?

" Some people might say my life is in a rut, I'm quite happy with what I got.

PAUL WELLER

"This is Jon, you know what to do." Beeeeeeeeeeeeeep.

Again?

I hung up. If I left a third message, I'd sound desperate. But I sort of was desperate. It was all kicking off at The Midget. The beer was flowing, the band was rocking, both barmaids were flirting. I was pretty sure I'd narrowed it down to the blonde, I just needed a wingman.

"Have you ever noticed that all the barmaids here are short?" asked Hank.

"She's not short, she's perfectly proportioned." I said.

"Is that why they call it The Midget?"

The band cranked out the first iconic cords of Going Underground. Tonight was going to blow the bloody doors off. I gave Jon one last thought; he'll be gutted to miss this. I shrugged it off and dived back unto the breach.

DRINKING IS FRIENDSHIP

If you venture out on the average Saturday night to the average watering hole in the average urban area you'll see a lot of people who seem to be enjoying themselves. But are they enjoying the alcohol or are they actually enjoying the night out? Is it the booze or the fact that they've finished work, they're with their mates and they're celebrating life? Have you ever wondered what they're enjoying, the situation or the alcohol?

Maybe it's both?

Flip it for a second. Would they enjoy partying if they weren't drinking? Probably not. They'd probably be miserable. But does that mean the alcohol brings joy? Not necessarily. Maybe it's the social pressure to drink, maybe that pressure would make them feel uncomfortable without a drink.

And that's something to consider. Is the benefit of drinking alcohol the fact that it removes the discomfort of not drinking?

The irritation is internal but it can come from outside influences. You must've felt it. There's something in that uneasiness. Thnk about it another way, do you get the same discomfort because you aren't allowed to smoke cocaine?

No? Then again, how many times do you get asked why you're not firing up the crack pipe?

Seriously, on a night out how many times do people say, "Come on, freebase!"?

 How often do you have to justify not smoking crack?

I'm guessing that never happens.

Now go into any pub in the country and order an apple juice. Hang around for long enough and someone will ask why you aren't drinking. Why is it that we must justify not drinking? It's literally the only drug on the planet where you have to explain why you aren't doing it.

Doesn't that seem, well, a bit strange?

The big illusion

Most people believe that alcohol is important, even crucial to the success of social events. Many people believe that alcohol is a major component of forging friendships. Now I'm going to go out on a limb here and say that's bollocks. It's what I like to call an illusion of truth. I like to call it that because that's what my dead smart neuroscientist mate Dr Lynda Shaw calls it.

An illusion of truth is something you believe because you've heard it a lot, even though it has been repeatedly demonstrated to be incorrect.

Let's look at a classic example. You probably believe that the Great Wall of China is visible from space. But why do you believe that? Have you been to space to check? You don't believe it because it's true – it's not – you believe it because you've heard it a lot.

It's not so bad when your illusory truth is about far eastern architecture, but what about alcohol? You probably believe that drinking helps you to socialise. You believe this despite the fact that it has rendered you unable to speak and caused you to throw up on people – not widely regarded as social characteristics. Yet you continue to believe that alcohol transforms you into smooth-talking, laugh-a-minute raconteur.

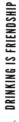

Insert fancy psychology name here

The illusory truth effect was first documented by Hasher, Goldstein and Toppino. They proved that people were more likely to consider something to be true based on how often they had heard it, rather than how likely it was to be true.

In short, if you keep hearing it you'll believe it – regardless of any evidence to the contrary. This is why the alcohol industry spends tens of billions of pounds every year telling you how great its product is. It's why they pay Roger Federer a tonne of money to have his picture taken with champagne. Bubbly booze plays no part in his success but because you keep seeing it you believe that it does.

As you have probably figured out, politicians know this too. That's why they keep repeating themselves: if they keep saying it, we start believing it. Why else do you think Putin spends so much time going on about how the west is out to get him? If he says it enough you'll believe it. Well, not you, you're smart, but the iron-headed Ivans who drink a bottle of vodka before work and vote Putin, they're genuinely buying it.

It's time to question what the alcohol companies have been telling you. It's time to pull back the curtain on the illusion of truth. Who knows, you might also start to listen to politicians with a new set of ears as well.

Friends like these

I'm going to level with you. My friends and I washed a lot of booze under a lot of bridges. For a couple of decades it was as if our relationship floated on ethanol.

But the waters were not always calm.

I remember one incident from my misspent youth. One of our housemates had made a curry, like properly, from scratch and everything. No takeaway, no cook-in sauces, real, honest to god culinary skills. We were impressed.

For about 10 minutes. Then we realised they'd used so much turmeric they stained all the plates yellow. What's the obvious thing to do in a situation like that? Ask them to give the plates a wash? Maybe with a bit of bicarb? Have a sensible discussion about it? All of those are great answers.

Unless you're drunk.

If you're drunk, then the logical solution is to put the offending plates in their bed.

Needless to say, this caused some recriminations. Needless to say, this wasn't conducive to a healthy and happy living environment. Needless to say, a lot of eggshells got trodden on, and not because of the hangovers.

I only mention it to reinforce the point that when we think about alcohol and friendship we have a huge blind spot. We think about the good bits, we think about the fun.

We tend to ignore the bad bits, the arguments, the stupid, thoughtless stuff we do to people who are supposed to be our mates. We ignore it and we certainly never admit that the behaviour is caused by alcohol. Honestly, do you think I'm the kind of person that would put dirty dishes in a mate's bed sober?

 It takes effort to ignore the fact that alcohol turns you into a spunktrumpet.

Look back on your life and think about how often alcohol has caused disagreements, arguments, falling outs, storming-offs and the end of friendships. No doubt you have examples.

Seriously, who punches their friend when they're sober? You have to be a proper bug-eyed nut-job to do that but add half a dozen beers and it happens every Saturday night.

HOW DID WE END UP THIS WAY?

Alcohol isn't magic party juice; it always dulls social occasions and often ruins them. Yet we believe that booze is the life and soul of the party. Why? Because we taught ourselves to connect social events with drinking.

 We taught ourselves to drink.

It seems like a strange way to think about it. Most people wouldn't say they learnt to drink. Yet you learnt to count, you learnt to drive, you learnt not to ask Noxious Nick why he's smiling. So why not say that you learnt to drink?

And the way you learnt it is intriguing. You used a more effective learning system than you'll ever see in school.

It may surprise you but parties are actually potent learning machines. Don't get too excited, parties aren't a substitute for revising for exams. I extensively tested that at University and it didn't work. Parties are just good at teaching one thing: you should drink at parties.

You remember the Tactical Change System, right? It's what you've been doing in the morning with your first cup of coffee.

TRIGGER
Something reminds you to carry out the behaviour.

ACTION

The behaviour itself.

CELEBRATION

Something positive that causes your brains to release particular chemicals that cements the learning.

The bad news is that the Tactical Change System has an evil twin brother, the accidental change system. It's basically the same but it teaches you to do stuff you don't really want to do. A party has every element of the accidental change system.

TRIGGER

The event reminds us to drink.

ACTION

We drink.

CELEBRATION

Whether we enjoy the party or not the alcohol floods our brains with chemicals. It's like a disco in your mind, celebrate good times, come on!

But that's not the end of it. The really clever bit is what happens after the celebration. Celebration, and alcohol, both release dopamine. You've heard of dopamine, right? Dopamine is a neurotransmitter and it's part of what makes us happy. That's the celebration bit. But it's also part of what helps us learn. That's the clever bit.

Because we have released dopamine into our head, our brain thinks to itself, "that was fun, let's do that some more". So our brains start to look out for other opportunities to grab some more sweet, sweet dopamine. That desire to repeat the experience is called tracking.

Partying

Let's apply that to the party. The event is the trigger that reminds us to drink. Drinking is the action. The enjoyable event, or the alcohol, creates the celebration, ie the dopamine. That creates the tracking that causes us to search out other similar events.

What you've created is an attention loop. The behaviour causes your brain to look out for more opportunities to perform the behaviour, which causes you to perform the behaviour again, which in turn causes your brain to look out for more opportunities.

The behaviour drives more of the behaviour. That's how we teach ourselves to connect parties with alcohol.

Tactical coffee

Incidentally, how are you getting on saying "Real Men Quit" with your first coffee?

If you're full lung shouting with your arms in the air, go you. If you've forgotten, consider this a gentle reminder. Maybe go and put that note on the kettle.

If you've read this far in one go, well done, but mate, at least grab a cup of something and have a stretch.

I'm not going to tell you how to read this book, if you've read this far then I trust you to get through the rest without training wheels. Read it however you want to. Read it on the train, read it on the bog, read it when you're on a Zoom call for work – don't forget to mute when you shout "real men quit".

What I will tell you to do is remember the Tactical Change System. Making that first cup of coffee is the trigger. Saying "Real Men Quit" to yourself is the action. Smiling is the celebration. Trigger. Action. Celebration. It's already starting to create the tracking. Your brain is more alert to your morning coffee. It's starting to look out for that sweet dopamine hit.

The behaviour is starting to drive the behaviour.

You're rewiring your brain. Go you! Your neurological electrical safety certificate is in the post. All you need to do is keep at it.

Spoiler alert: the accidental change system taught you to drink. Double spoiler alert: its good-looking brother, the Tactical Change System, will teach you not to.

 The way in is the way out.

These systems are just doors. Any door that lets you in can let you out again.

" No more will my green sea go turn a deeper blue.

MICK JAGGER AND KEITH RICHARDS

There was a heavy clunk as she answered, a kind of telephonic note of foreboding.

"Hi, I've been trying to get through to Jon but he's not answering his phone?"

"Oh." His mother sounded worried.

Silence.

"Is something the matter?" I asked.

"He's..." Uncertainty. "...in hospital."

It hit me like a George Foreman body shot. The wind thumped out of me – this was no rope-a-dope.

I knew he'd been ill last summer. I didn't know what the problem had been. We're blokes, we never talked about that sort of thing. Let's be clear, I'm not a totally self-obsessed monster. I did ask. But Jon brushed it aside. He drowned it with the perfect Tom Collins, drunk out of pint glasses.

I assumed he was over it.

Clearly not.

The only information I could get from his mum was something about his pancreas. He was in intensive care.

What was Jon doing in intensive care?

DRINKING RELIEVES STRESS

Has this ever happened to you? You wake up late. You feel ropey. But you power through. You make it to work, maybe on time, maybe not. You start the day on the back foot – it doesn't improve. Your boss is idiotic, everything is unnecessarily tough, things break. By the time you finish work you're so stressed you feel like King Harold at the end of the battle of Hastings.

You recognise that, right? What do you do after a day like that? Drink? A lot? That's the natural reaction. One of the main illusions about drinking is that it helps you deal with stress. But how does it do that?

Let's consider why the above example was stressful. There are some genuinely annoying elements. Stupid bosses are stressful. Tasks that push you to the limit of your ability are stressful. Being asked to do too much is stressful. Being expected to complete a task you lack the resources to complete is stressful. Trying to defeat a rampaging Norman army is stressful. All of those are genuinely aggravating things.

Now ask yourself this question: how does alcohol help you with any of those? Will it increase your boss's IQ? Will it expand your ability? Will it reduce your workload? Will it provide you with additional resources? Will it change the fact that the Norman military package is vastly superior to Anglo-Saxon weapon systems?

Obviously not. Whether you drink or not, everything that's wrong with your job will still be there tomorrow. Alcohol doesn't help with genuinely stressful stuff. In fact, with two minutes and not much imagination you could figure out how alcohol actually reduces your ability, makes your workload *seem* larger, makes your resources *feel* smaller and if any of your colleagues have been drinking, then it'll be short tempers all round. Statistically, you're even more likely to get an arrow in the eye socket.

Alcohol doesn't solve problems

But there's much more to bad days than just the stuff that you can't do anything about. What about waking up late? What about making it into work with seconds to spare? What about feeling tired all day? What about struggling to focus? What about that low-level unhappy feeling that you've been carrying around for so long that you've started to think it's just life? What about the battle of Stamford Bridge?

That isn't life. That isn't who you are. That isn't because you're not a morning person. That's alcohol.

 All that additional stress comes from drinking.

Except the battle of Stamford Bridge. That was the bloody Vikings fault.

Even if you're not prepared to give up on the idea that alcohol helps *deal* with stress you're going to have to face up to the fact that alcohol *causes* stress. It then becomes more of a maths puzzle – how much stress does alcohol have to relieve to make up for the stress that it causes?

A tapestry of stress

I'm wondering: are you thinking, "wow, Duncan, you've just blown my mind. It's like I've taken the blue pill and I can see the matrix for what it really is."

Maybe that's exactly what you're thinking, but there's a part of your brain that wants to disagree. Don't worry, that's not unusual. Part of you is thinking "alcohol is my release mechanism, it helps me to escape from the crap of everyday life". I get that. I said that for years. What you're saying is that alcohol helps you run away from your problems.

Now think about the geography of that statement for a moment. Running away is about putting some distance between you and something else. If you're running away from zombies or FBI agents you expect to get further away from them. If you don't move you end up as another zombie, or as a docile cog in the American industrial complex, which is pretty much the same thing.

Does drinking help you get further away from your problems? Not a millimetre. The problems are still there, you're still there, nothing has moved. You aren't running away from your problems. You're running around them and around them and around them – all day, every day.

And man is that stressful.

The cycle of conformity

Running around your problems is a cycle. You wake up. You feel bad. You have a bad day. You drink. You wake up. You feel bad. You have a bad… On and on. You recognise that, right? Maybe you didn't realise that it was a cycle, Maybe you thought it was a life.

Look, you have pain in your life – even if it's something as comparatively minor as a bad day – and there are many things that can cause pain. That pain causes you to drink alcohol. Then the next day, or sometimes even while you are doing it, you begin to regret it. That regret causes you more pain. Pain. Behaviour. Regret. More pain.

That's what we do. I did it for twenty years. Many do it for longer – some do it for a lifetime. I don't know how long you've been doing it for, but my guess is long enough. The good news is that you're going to stop this cycle. The first step is to realise that it's a cycle, which you have done. You're officially challenging your assumption. You're a belief disposal machine. Oorah marine.

If only King Harold had known

But while we're in that cycle what do we say? We take any opportunity to tell people how much alcohol helps us to deal with stress. And there it is again, the illusion of truth. The alcohol industry has been peddling this myth for years, but the really surprising thing is that they're still getting away with it.

During the global pandemic an American discount booze store used this slogan "Liquor. Cheaper than therapy." Wow, what a valuable public service that they are offering. Maybe they should get an award.

What's worse are the memes that burn across social media like wildfire during a drought. I like the one with Gorgu (baby Yoda) saying "Hide from your kids and drink wine you must". Or one employee asking "how come you never stress out at work?" while the other is pouring brandy into his coffee. Or "don't forget alcohol helps to remove the stress. The bra, the panties and many other problems."

You've got to wonder who comes up with these things. Is there an office deep in the heart of an alco-giant dedicated to developing frighteningly inappropriate memes for us to share like inebriated sheep?

Sadly, I doubt it. It seems all too plausible that we're happy to reinforce the illusion of truth ourselves. After all, it's not the alcohol industry that's encouraging people to buy baby-grows with "It's beer o'clock" on them. That's not even the worst of it. I saw one with "you can't drink all day if you don't start in the morning" written on it.

And some people think I overestimate the amount we're bombarded with these messages. I'm not exaggerating. As soon as you are able to listen you start to hear things about alcohol which aren't true. They start in on the illusion of truth early. Heck, they even write it on your baby-grow.

Finding the balance

Before we move on, I want to hammer this nail all the way in. Deep in the dark recess of your skull, the belief that alcohol reduces your stress probably still lingers.

Yet you can accept that some, and perhaps a lot, of the stress in your life is actually caused by drinking alcohol.

Nevertheless, you still cling to the idea that it relieves stress. We'll get into that later. But just for the moment let's pretend that it's true. Let's pretend that alcohol really does reduce stress.

Ask yourself how much stress would alcohol need to relieve just to get it back to normal? What would it need to do to just wipe out the stress it causes? Think of all the issues it causes and then imagine how much relief it would need to bring just to get back to net stress zero.

Even to achieve a balance of stress caused to stress relieved, it would have to be a miracle drug. Which means the question now becomes...

Is alcohol a miracle drug?

DRINKING MAKES YOU SEXY

I t doesn't take more than a cursory glance at alcohol advertising to spot what they're up to. Images of sexy women abound. It's so entrenched ad people have an expression for it, the three Bs: blonde, bikini, bottle.

It's so obvious, so pervasive, so completely a part of the booze-advertising programme that I'm not going to patronise you by laying it on thick. But I am going to share my all-time favourite alco-ad, this beauty.

HOW TO DRAW IN FOUR EASY STEPS

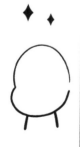   

What are they saying? In essence, she's ugly so get drunk and she'll look like the Mona Lisa. Simple? Yes. Effective? Probably. Crass? Basically.

Let's stare it in the face. You've probably woken up in the wrong bed or next to the wrong person. It's a dreadful feeling; the last thing you want to do is look at them. It's a cold realisation that just because they were blurry last night doesn't make them good looking this morning. Try as you might, you just can't remember their name. You pretend to be asleep and hope they slip away. You contemplate pretending to be dead.

Once you pop...

That feeling of dread, regret and shame – that wasn't in the adverts, was it? The adverts are full of beautiful semi-naked women, implying that your Saturday night is going to be like that. That's the illusion of truth.

I have to admit, thus far I've rather assumed that you find women attractive. That's not because I have strong opinions of who you should have sexy time with. I talk about coffee because I like coffee. If you like tea, it's cool and I assume you have enough wit and imagination to think your way around my frequent references to coffee. Just imaging whatever ticks your boxes.

It probably doesn't surprise you to know that I think sex is like firing a rifle. There are two elements to shooting: picking the shot and hitting the target. In the same way if you want to have sex, you have to find a willing partner (pick the shot) and then you have to perform the act (hit the target). They're two separate but related phases.

Let's consider how alcohol helps you fire your gun.

Picking the shot

What attributes do you imagine women find attractive? You could waste days on Google looking it up. Maybe you have.

A survey of internet-based advice pages is probably going to come up with something like confidence, kindness, humour and honesty. When pushed, the authors of these lists would probably agree that being able to stand upright, not slurring your words or having kebab down your shirt are also important but they probably considered those to be a given.

Now let's consider the effects of alcohol.

CONFIDENCE

Will alcohol make you more confident? Well, maybe you'll get a surge of boldness but it quickly tips into over-confidence. Which is a polite way of saying obnoxious arrogance – not that attractive.

KINDNESS

I don't know about you, but alcohol never made me kind. It only made me care about myself. It made me Gollum, the next drink becoming "my precious". Pathetic desperation is not exactly sexy.

HUMOUR

Does alcohol make you funny? It makes you think you're funny, which is the opposite of funny. And it can make you hilarious by turning you into an object of ridicule. Not a good look.

HONEST

Honest? Seriously? Last time a medical professional asked you how much you drink, did you tell the truth? Don't worry, it's not your fault. Neurological studies have shown that alcohol shrinks the bit of your brain responsible for honesty.

If you have any attractive qualities before you drink then alcohol is going to reduce them. And if you aren't confident, kind, funny and honest you're screwed. Actually, you're not getting screwed and no amount of alcohol is going to help. Let's face it, after six pints you're far more likely to be into the territory of bumping into stuff and pissing yourself.

DRINKING MAKES YOU SEXY

69

Alcohol only makes you more attractive to people if they're drunk. In other words, it's only if their judgement is as impaired as yours that you'll look even remotely attractive.

Hitting the target

No one wants the perfect shot lined up in the sights only to misfire. That would be embarrassing. How does alcohol help you shoot straight?

As Shakespeare pointed out "it provokes the desire, but it takes away the performance." And he said that without the benefit of modern medicine, which has found that, among heavy drinkers, 72% suffered from at least one sexual problem. Top of the list was premature ejaculation and erectile dysfunction.

Maybe you're smiling because you think sex lasts longer when you're drunk. That would be due to alcohol's desensitising effect. Think about that for a second – you're telling me that an experience is enhanced because you can't sense it? Would you like to eat more but not taste it?

I'm not trying to overemphasise the negative effects of alcohol in the hope that it puts you off. I know it won't. I'm trying to point out the gap between the adverts and the reality. In fact, I'm trying to get you to see that there is a gap between what you believe about alcohol and your own experience of it.

That said, I feel honour-bound to point out that beer contains phytoestrogen and prolactin. Both of which increase oestrogen and reduce testosterone. Goodbye manliness. Hello man-boobliness.

Not all fun and games

All jokes aside, drinking alcohol impairs your judgement.

Therein lies the problem. You're hoping to convince someone to sleep with you based on their impaired judgement. At best this isn't a strategy to build a long-term relationship. Maybe you're not looking for a long-term relationship – that's cool, but what will your conquest think once their judgement returns to normal?

They'll feel bad. Which is interesting, isn't it, because that's probably how you're going to feel too. That wasn't what the advert was offering, was it?

You know about feeling bad because you've done stupid things when drunk. It might have been a tattoo or chilli sauce or going to a terrible nightclub, even though you know no club on the Isle of Wight is ever worth the entry fee. Whatever it was, I imagine you regretted it in the morning.

Alcohol blurs your judgement so you do things that you wouldn't normally do. I get that. I've done more than my fair share of stupid stuff. Luckily, I got away with it. I only got kicked out of clubs, told off by the police and busted by my girlfriend.

I managed to avoid any serious legal problems. Yet there's a very dark side to drinking, particularly if you mix it with sex. Alcohol is a major risk factor in sexual assault and domestic abuse. Studies show that alcohol is involved in around half of all sexual assaults.

Now I'm not saying that if you drink you'll become a rapist, but the fact is that mixing alcohol and sex is rolling the dice.

In the cold light of day, you can see that if a woman is not in a position to wholeheartedly say yes, then it's a no. When you're sober you can understand consent and all the subtle elements of communication that go into it. Are you able to do that after eight pints? Even after four?

Look, I'm sure you're a nice guy who treats women with respect, but these are the risks we run when we drink. We run them because drinking blurs our judgement, because it fills us full of confidence and passion. It doesn't say it in the adverts, but alcohol is what makes normal, sensible men do stupid things.

 Too many guys have gone out for a drink and ended up in a cell.

That's all truth, no illusion.

What it says on the tin

Consider for a second, are you getting what the booze companies say they're giving you? Is drinking some bikini-clad paradise or is it something quite different, almost the opposite?

Maybe you remember the Ronseal ads. The no-nonsense manly man shouting "It does what it says on the tin". Well let's apply that to alcohol. Does it do what it says on the tin?

Maybe if the bottle had "Limp dick. Slurred words. Just plain annoying." emblazoned on it, then we could trust the alcohol industry. Then it would do what it says on the tin.

"You just keep me hanging on.

LOU REED

I stretched the last strand of parcel tape over the box. It wasn't going to win any design awards but it would make it through the postal system, probably.

We had cobbled together a care package for Jon. We did it with love and diligence. Bits, bobs, sweets, sours, a Simpson's pencil sharpener, a pack of Top Trumps and a truly ugly plastic doll.

"Let's get this in the post." I said, with the determination of botulism.

"Man, there's always a massive queue at the post office this late in the afternoon." Hank whined.

I thought about that for a second. Where had Hank got his intel about the post office's customer flow?

"We can do it in the morning, it's our duty to go to the pub." He smiled.

"Really?"

"Emancipate yourself from mental slavery, man. We aren't just dumb cogs in the catastrophic machine, we're warriors, revolutionaries, freedom fighters."

"We are?"

"Hell yeah, it's our duty to stick it to the postman." He solemnly raised a fist.

I was still a little sceptical, but I knew there was no stopping him when he got like this.

"Power to the pint glass," he shouted.

"I'll get my beret."

"I wouldn't, it's a bit Frank Spencer."

As I grabbed my keys there was a little something, a miniscule tickle behind my ribs that was saying this wasn't right. It was short lived. It soon gave way to uncertainty as to where I'd put my wallet.

*

What sort of person goes out drinking rather than sending something to their friend in intensive care? I've asked that question again and again.

What difference could it have made if the parcel had arrived a little earlier? What might my care have done? The regret burnt. The sorrow that I chose the pub over the post office seared me to the core, it fricasseed my soul. It had not been worth it. How could it ever have been worth it?

Jon was dead before the parcel arrived.

THE EMERGENCY EXIT

arc Lewis, who's a rock'n'roll neurologist – yes, that's a real job title – once said drinking is like a house with many doors. There are many ways into the house. The bad news is that it's very easy to enter, but the good news is that doors work in two directions. Getting out is easy.

 The way in is the way out

You can walk through any door at any time. But before you do that you need to completely understand how you walked in in the first place. How did you learn to drink?

Passing the bar exam

We've already thought about how we taught ourselves to drink. We've already seen how to use the accidental change system to learn the skill of boozing.

TRIGGER

A party.

ACTION

A drink.

CELEBRATION

Laughter, dancing and maybe even kissing.

But that doesn't explain everything. It's not like you turned up at the party and said, "What is this strange brown, gaseous and slightly bitter drink?" You already knew what beer was and you already had plenty of ideas about it. How did you get those?

You were exposed to alcohol thousands of times before that party. You watched your family drink, you watched people on TV drink, you heard songs about drinking, you saw sportsmen spraying champagne. You get the idea. It's everywhere.

We were watching TV

But to prove a point let's make it really simple. Imagine you watched a beer advert. Your impressionable, hormone-filled mind thought "wow, if I drank beer I could hook-up with sexy women". You pictured yourself doing something with those women.

TRIGGER

An advert.

ACTION

You connect beer with girls.

CELEBRATION

Imagine girls. Get hard-on.

That created the tracking, but the interesting point is that you don't start tracking beer ads – no, you're looking out for beer. That's the first step to learning to drink.

I want to be clear – I don't think that you actually watched a beer ad and said, out loud, "Wow, if I drank beer I could hook-up with sexy women". The process is clearly more subtle than that. I've just tried to explain a complex system of neurological wiring in a hopefully memorable way.

And what did you do after you'd seen the advert and rewired your brain a bit?

You went to a party. You saw beer. You drank beer. You went home with the most beautiful woman at the party. Trigger, a party. Action, a beer. Celebration, a spot of copulation. That's some powerful tracking, brother.

But wait...

It's just about possible that you didn't end your first night of drinking in the mad throws of passion with the model-hot girl of your dreams. That's just about believable.

My first experience of drinking was embarrassing. Maybe your first experience of alcohol was likewise, too full of vomit to fit in a hardcore shagathon. Maybe you're thinking that it shouldn't have worked for you. Don't worry, you can still learn to love beer in such a situation.

Remember dopamine? You get that from the alcohol so even a seemingly bad experience can create the tracking.

 Dopamine teaches: everything else is detail.

Keep your eyes on the door

You understand how you got into this mess. You appreciate it was dopamine that did it.

And you're becoming the master of dopamine: coffee is the trigger, "Real Men Quit!" is the action. The smile is the celebration.

Beneath the celebration is the dopamine. Remember that smiling dumps a bunch of happy chemicals into your head, whether you are happy or not.

Trigger. Action. Celebration. Dopamine. Tracking. Bang! Tactical Change.

The dopamine makes you pay attention to the coffee. The dopamine creates the learning. The dopamine makes it an attention loop. Believe me, that's what got you into this mess and it's what's going to get you out again.

WHY DID YOU END UP LIKE THIS?

Do you think you're in control of your drinking? If the answer is yes, then the question becomes why the hell do you keep doing it? You can't have read this much of the book whistling to yourself and thinking, "that sounds terrible but in my perfumed garden we sip sweet nectar while admiring the flowers and discussing the poetry of John Keats". You must have some desire to at least cut back. If you're in control, then why don't you?

One of two things must be true: one, you have no desire to stop drinking and you're only reading this book because the jokes keep coming. True, they aren't original, but they are punctual. Or two, you have the desire to change your drinking but you lack the control to do it. As much as you like a laugh, I expect it's the latter.

 You cannot control your drinking.

That's no surprise. No one is really in control of their drinking. We all appear to be in control because we all appear to be making the choice to drink. But that just lands us back where we started. If you have the choice and you want to stop, just choose not to drink.

You tried choosing not to drink, right? I tried it. I tried it every morning. I would wake up and choose not to drink that day. But by the evening I seemed to have changed my choice.

Let's face it, the freedom you have is like the freedom Russian people have. They can support the regime or take a fifteen-year break in a snow and razor-wire holiday camp with a seriously shouty concierge. If they choose their principles, they get the pain.

Which is just like drinking. You can keep doing it even though it conflicts with who you really are. Or you can stop – but at the moment you think barbed wire, dehumanisation and too much attention from guys who look like *The I-Spy Book of Prison Tattoos* are apt metaphors for what happens when you do. At the moment you think that giving up the sauce will land you in a world of pain.

But there's a glimmer of hope. The idea that stopping drinking has to feel like you're surrounded by Kalashnikov-waving sociopaths with furry hats might not be true. You think it's hard to quit, but is it? Could that be an illusion of truth too?

Fairground attraction

Drinking is like a rollercoaster. I don't mean that you feel dizzy and throw up – you're not a teenager anymore. No, I mean that if you do it for long enough drinking ends up feeling like you're stuck on a rollercoaster.

At the start, you stand by the ride and you see all of the people screaming with pleasure. It's exciting, exhilarating, even a bit dangerous. You think to yourself, "I wanna go on that!".

You get on the rollercoaster. Down comes the padded metal strap and pins you to your seat. The ride cranks into action. You're nervous as it clicks up the big hill. You reach the highest point on the track. Time seems to stand still. Then woosh. You're speeding, racing, banking, turning tightly, looping the loop and generally having a fine old time.

You enjoy it. It's exhilarating. You think to yourself, "I have made a wise decision, this is great".

The carriage brakes at the platform. Brilliant. This is the point where you expect the strap to release you so you can grab an overpriced hotdog. But think about it – are you in control? Do you decide if the strap goes up?

No, the system decides whether or not you get off. There's a computer programme that controls the rollercoaster and it determines if you get off the ride.

Nevertheless, up goes the strap and off you get. Of course, the ride has given your brain a powerful hit of dopamine. You've given over a little corner of your brain to the connection between roller coasters and fun.

You go and shy some coconuts, but you also keep half an eye on the rollercoaster. Obviously, you get on it again. Again, it's exciting. It's fun. It's madly pumping dopamine into your skull. You get to the end of the track. But this time the padded metal strap doesn't go up. And you have no control over that.

You're staying on the rollercoaster. Round you go again. It's still enjoyable. You get back to the station. The strap remains in place.

Round you go again. On and on. But now you aren't enjoying it. Now it is just making you feel dizzy and sick. You want to get off, but that strap won't budge. You're trapped on the rollercoaster.

Choose life

You chose to get on to the ride, but you never chose to stay on it when you stopped enjoying it. You got on it because it looked like fun, and maybe it was to start with. Sooner or later you got trapped on the rollercoaster.

Alcohol is exactly the same. You chose to have those first few drinks but one day it stops being a choice and starts to feel like an oppressive collar pining you into the seat, pinning you into a constantly moving, constantly spinning nightmare. Much as you want to, you can't get off.

Round and round you go. At some point, a point that you never recognised, you lost the ability to get off the rollercoaster that is alcohol.

You could argue that you lost control of drinking at the point when you changed the structure of your brain, or when your body seemed to need alcohol, or when your mind felt dependent on it. Or you could argue that you lost control when you took your first drink. It doesn't really matter.

 It doesn't matter when you lost control, it matters what you do about it.

Twice the fun

Here's the plan. Dopamine got you into this mess. Dopamine is going to get you out of it too. But only if you understand it – don't start Googling dopamine pills. You need to understand how to get your brain to make it for you.

So far I've talked about celebrations causing dopamine release but there's more to it. The trigger releases dopamine too.

But you know this because you know about anticipation. And you've heard of Pavlov. I bet you're thinking, "yeah, he was that Russian fella who trained dogs to salivate at the sound of a bell."

You're partly right. The bell bit is an illusion of truth – it's something you think you know because you've heard it a lot. Pavlov actually used a variety of things, like a metronome, a harmonium, a buzzer, and an electric shock (what is it with scientists and electric shocks?). Please promise me you'll never agree to take part in a psychology study.

Anyhow, you're right about the salivating bit. The dogs had an uncontrollable physical response not to food but to what they thought would bring the food. Pavlov first noticed that they drooled at the chap in the lab coat who brought the food. You're right enough.

 We often respond not to the action but to the trigger.

Double the molecules

There are two powerful dopamine hits during the process. It starts with the trigger, with the anticipation of what's coming. And it peaks with celebration.

That's why you start looking out for the trigger, not just the action. That's the powerful engine that drives the tracking.

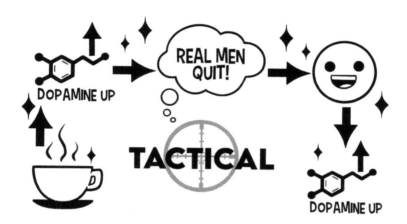

Maybe this intuitively makes sense to you. Maybe you're just like I used to be – maybe you feel the relief not when you have your first drink but when you know you're going to get your first drink. I always got that first dopamine hit when I was queuing up in the shop to buy some wine. My brain would give me that little reward because it knew the bigger reward was coming.

Which is an interesting point. Your body is *not* dependent on the chemicals in the alcohol, not as such. I mean alcohol is powerful stuff but there's no drug that's so powerful it will create an effect *before* you consume it.

 Your problem is in your brain, not in the bottle.

We'll look at the effect alcohol has on your brain chemistry in more detail later. For now, ask yourself whether you're choosing to drink, or if you're locked into the dopamine rollercoaster?

> ## " After changes upon changes, we are more or less the same.

PAUL SIMON

The sun should not have shone. There was no reason for the weather to be good – it was a bright face sneering at a blunt day.

There should have been thunder, lightning, wind and rain. It should have been full of riddle and witchery, dark like Hecate's eyes. It should have bubbled with toil and trouble. We should have met upon a heath not a picture-perfect village churchyard with scenic trees and artistic moss.

Jon was buried in a wicker coffin. It creaked the whole way down, a pitch that found a direct line from my ears to my pain. The kind of haunting sound that makes you sweat while chilling your blood. The noise that dread is made of.

I lined up with everyone else, taking our turn to throw a flower onto his casket and say goodbye in our own way. As I stood over the grave, I paused, unsure whether to laugh or cry. I wanted neither. I wanted the black.

Instead of feeling I thought a ridiculous thought. "When I get to hell, I'm going to kick your arse."

*

Oblivious, I found my way into Andy's car. He'd rolled a joint which we used to waste the time between the burial and the wake. Which we used to waste ourselves.

"Do you remember that time..." he started to ask.

I didn't hear the story. Doubtless it was a good one, but the remembrance of memories had catapulted me into my own cavern of recollection. Because I really do remember the time...

The time he transformed a pizza box into a perplexing and frightening mask.

The time we found him sleeping on a ringing alarm clock.

The first time I heard him play piano.

When we tried to attract Husain's attention with starting pistols rather than his doorbell.

How he would beat the living daylights out of me on a computer game then recoil in terror if I somehow managed to lay a blow on him.

Stuttering through the woods with a stolen barstool and attempting to look casual as someone walked past.

Sitting on a gently rocking sofa trying to ignore the fact that the people in the bed behind us were having sex.

Mashed potato.

The first time that we heard the birds singing and realised we'd talked all night and it was dawn.

I remember every night it happened.

I was brought back to the present as Andy notched up the volume on the stereo. I knew the track; it was by Luke Vibert but I never knew the title. We just called it the "everything is going to be alright" song.

This time, I wasn't so sure.

TIME FOR A CHANGE

You feel that things have got to change, right? It's dawning on you that it's time to put an end to your days of drinking in the darkness, yes? In the heart of your heart you've decided to abandon the vagabond life, the life of outlaw chicanery. You've worked out it's time to live like a normal(ish) human, with a normal(ish) life.

There are many things that could have taken you to this point. Like me you could have lost someone close to you. Or you could have destroyed a relationship that was important. It could even be something good. A pregnancy, or a promotion, and it should be pure joy but it's tainted by the fact that you're still drinking. Worse still, you know that these two courses will inevitably collide. Pretty soon your success and your drinking are going to crash together and people you care about are going to get hurt.

It's like a grave is opening up before you, forcing you to wonder what the heck you're doing with your life. However you got to the cemetery, you're starting to see that you don't enjoy drinking. And you know what?

 If you don't enjoy alcohol now, you never will.

I'm no different from you. I'm not special. If you don't believe me, ask my wife. I'm just an ordinary guy. True, I've done a bit more work. True, I'm a bit further down the path but that's not because I'm extraordinary. I just walked through a door.

Exactly what brought you to this point does not matter. Who you are does not matter. Like Marc Lewis says, drinking is a house with many doors. No matter which door leads you in, any door can take you out.

You too can walk through the door to the life you want, the life you need, the life you deserve.

Once a drinker always a drinker

But maybe you think that you're a drinker; it's who you are. Maybe you think you have about as much chance of changing that as you do of changing the size of your cock. You've seen those ads and you're pretty sure they lie.

Maybe you don't believe that you're capable of living a normal life. Maybe you don't think you deserve a better life. Maybe you don't believe that it can ever be different.

Life is made up of a series of small actions. Think about it; winning the World Cup ultimately comes down to three things: run, kick, repeat. Sure, we only notice Geoff Hurst lumping it into the back of the net – we only see one kick. Yet what got the English national team to that point on that fateful day? Run, kick, repeat. Run, kick, repeat. Run, kick, repeat. Literally thousands of other kicks and miles of running got Sir Geoff to that point where one kick could make sure it was all over. It's the small actions, the ones that seem inconsequential on their own, they're the ones that add up to success.

Incidentally, every time England loses a football match it's also because of small actions: run, kick, penalties.

Pretty soon, I'm going to share the small actions you need to take to get free from alcohol. It's time to create some momentum and live the life you were born to live. The small actions are the change.

The good news is you've already changed.

Simply by learning to say "Real Men Quit" with your first coffee you've changed. You've learnt to behave in a different way. I know that it might seem trivial, but it's the key to getting free.

And you will get free. It might sound like I have more confidence in your abilities than you do. Maybe I do. I'm prepared to lend you my confidence if you like. You can borrow it for the next few chapters until you get a little more of your own. So grin, grin like you've already made it, grin like it's already done, grin like you're already free. You're all over this.

You are here?

We're coming to the end of this section, and it seems like a good idea to pause and check out where you've got to. I'm damn sure you have challenged your assumptions about alcohol. But have you been blowing up some outdated beliefs?

In an absolutely ideal world you'd believe, deep down in the wellspring of your being, that alcohol does not serve you. That it doesn't provide you with any benefits and in fact it never has. That it's not a part of who you are – in fact, it gets in the way of being your true self.

Once you realise that you no longer want to drink, not drinking is simple. As Paul Tillich once said, "Without temptation there is no desire".

 If you don't want something, you don't struggle when you don't have it.

Remember the first bullet-hole of change is to challenge your assumptions. The first step to a new way of living is to challenge everything you believe about alcohol.

All we've tried to do in this section is move your beliefs a bit, somewhat alter your attitude and lose your illusions down the back of the sofa. This new solid base of belief is what we're going to build on.

Maybe you don't think you're there yet. That's cool. If you can acknowledge that much of what you've been told about alcohol doesn't match up with your experience then you're OK. If you're starting to

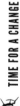

blow up the beliefs that underlie your drinking, you're on the right track. If you're starting to see the illusion of truth for what it is then you're walking in the right direction.

And in that direction lies the golden city of energy, focus, peace, strength, happiness and really, really good sex.

Keep marching, comrade.

TIME FOR A CHANGE

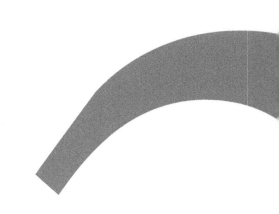

SECTION 2

Change Your Thoughts

" They want to be pirates but the sea is not calm.

Owen, Fox, Segs and Ruffy

The wake was getting lively, a lot of party people doing what they knew how to do. They had come from all over. They had travelled to show that they loved him. The various facets of Jon's life all came together. They should have formed a diamond but it felt more like coal dust.

"This wine is awful," Andy pointed out.

I hadn't noticed.

Another drink was pushed into my hand. "It's what he would have wanted" was shouted over the noise which was reaching nightclub levels.

"Yes", I thought, "not exactly what he needed though."

I got very drunk.

*

The countryside rolled past the way only a train-track landscape does. Trees, sheep, hills, houses, bushes, they carried on as normal, as if they'd entered some twilight zone of unawareness.

I was the captain of a small ship in that large storm. The horizon was lost in the skyscraping waves; the skiff kept bobbing, I kept praying, bobbing and praying in the neverending gale. It was the kind of on-slaught that just won't go away.

I wanted to scream out, is this it? Is this my life? Am I destined to endlessly seesaw in the tumult? Am I bound to drift from squall to squall to squall to squall with never a respite?

94

Or could there be a harbour? Could I make it to the land? Was there a chance I could live like everyone else? Do the things that normal people do, the things that I'd been raised to do, trained to do?

I rubbed my eyes and tried to clear the mental gale.

There must have been other people on the train but at that moment I was totally alone. Solitary, singular, trapped in my own head. Trapped in a cyclone of obligation and desire. Do I rove like Jon? Do I seek the storm and call it calm?

Or do I head for land, hang up my oilskins and live the disappointing life of a shipwrecked Jack Tar? Forever yearning to find my shipmates?

The countryside rolled past. The train forged onwards. The world turned oblivious.

*

Nothing changed after Jon's death. Hank and I still partied. I still got nowhere with the barmaids at The Midget. If anything, I drank more. But something inside of me yearned for different.

Right down at the core I knew that the drinking needed to stop. I knew that this behaviour had to have its limits. I knew that one day I must sort out my life, smarten up my act and start to live upon the land.

A part of me felt that, knew that, it was vital to live with my feet rooted into the earth, to bow to the authority of the man, to become a good little citizen.

But not yet.

Because I just couldn't quit being a weather-driven mariner. I wanted a little more high-seas hi-jinks. A little more time living the pirate's life of aromatic rum, full-bottomed wenches and wine-dark seas. I wanted to walk in foreign sand just a little longer.

Change was on the horizon. It was coming. But not today. Please, not today.

WHY REAL MEN QUIT

Seriously, who are you? There are many answers to that question. At a guess you're a man. Which means you're also a son, maybe a brother, a husband, even a father. You're certainly a friend. And you obviously have a playful sense of humour and great taste in books. After that I'll only make one more guess.

You're a drinker. There are so many things that are different about us but we share one thing. We're drinkers. Which means I'll go further with my guess; you have a problem with drinking. Just like I had, and millions of men do. And part of that problem is identity.

Do you think that being a drinker is a part of who you are? Do you think that even if you don't drink, you'll still be a drinker, just a drinker that isn't allowed to drink? I get that, I used to feel that way. Particularly if something stupid like driving or operating heavy machinery prevented me from drinking. How I felt like a drinker that couldn't drink.

I lost control of alcohol. True, if you'd have glanced at my life, you would have thought that I was in control. Heck, if you'd asked, I would have sworn blind I was in control. But I wasn't – every decision, every action, practically every thought was soaked in alcohol. If I was going out, I'd make sure I'd be back before the off-licence closed. If I was going away, I'd make sure I had enough booze with me. Part of me would be desperate for my wife to go to bed because it felt easier drinking alone. I wasn't in control of my thoughts and actions, alcohol was.

I was on that rollercoaster.

How about you? You're definitely a drinker. You're probably prepared to accept that you have a bit of an issue. But are you in control? Or are you on the rollercoaster too? Are you pinned down by the padded metal strap wondering when everything is just going to stop spinning for a minute or two?

There are no alcoholics

In the medical profession they don't use the term alcoholic, they talk about people who are dependent on alcohol. Let's think about that for a second. Dependent on alcohol. Do you feel like you depend on alcohol?

I'd guess that you can get out of bed without reaching for a drink, which means you think you don't depend on alcohol. But all that actually means is that you don't depend on it to get out of bed. Can you socialise without it? Can you handle stress without it? Can you have fun without it? Can you meet new people without it? Can you tolerate your mother-in-law without it? Sure, you can get through the day without a drink. But what about the evening?

If you need alcohol to have a good time, if you need a drink to handle stress, if you can't get through life without it then you *are* dependent on it.

I'll admit that you aren't as dependent as someone who requires a drink first thing in the morning, but you do depend on it to make your life work. Which means it's merely a matter of degrees. You currently only depend on it to get through social events but the logical conclusion of the path you're on is putting vodka on your cornflakes.

I know that sounds extreme and you probably baulk at the suggestion that you'll ever get to the point where you're doing the a.m. drinking thing. But surely you can see that it's the road you're on. You haven't driven to where the tarmac gives way to the ragged canyon and the long drop but isn't it simply a matter of time?

Look, no one wants to go to Slough. No one in the right mind would choose to go there. But if you spend enough time driving down the A4 you will end up in Slough. And morning drinking is even worse than Slough on a wet Monday.

What you have to realise is that you're travelling in a direction. You aren't miraculously going to do a 180. It won't magically get better. You won't suddenly start drinking less. You will only ever drink more and more. It will only ever take you down the road to Slough.

Maybe you think you're different.

I hate to break it to you but you're not. You're just like the rest of us. You may be in a different chair, in a different house, in a different city but you have the same poison in your glass and the same bullshit in your head.

 You're one of us, brother.

Not who but who?

The question isn't who are you: the question is, who do you want to be?

Do you want to be the vagabond skulking around the forest raiding the people of the village or scrounging up their scraps with only a cask of ale to get you through the cold and lonely night?

Or do you want to be a citizen? Not one of the boring ones who go on about how his hovel has risen in value again this quarter and how he's thinking about buying shares in the shire-horse business. No, you're more likely to want to start a shire-horse business or build a block of luxury hovels. Maybe you want to be a minstrel or a bard. Maybe you want to be mayor or even the king. Heck, you might be the guy that invents the crypto-groat.

I get that. I love the fact that you have spirit, that you won't settle for normal, that you want to change the world and if that involves making a cartload of money then so be it. The point is when you look in the mirror and wonder about what you might become, I doubt that reclusive, half-cut vagabond is on the list.

And if you've read this far I'm willing to guess that part of you is worried that this is how you'll end up. Which leads us to the real question: are you going to stop drinking for good?

Look, I'm not going to tell you what to do. I've only managed to be the boss of me for the last eight and a bit years; it seems a bit strong if I try to be the boss of you too. The decision is ultimately yours. The choice will always be yours but the danger of buying this book is that it subjects you to my rogue opinions, so here they are.

Stop drinking. Forever.

Part of you probably thinks that's bad news. Don't panic. I'm not telling you to stop right now, you have a few more chapters to get used to the idea. So take a moment to contemplate what a non-drinking you might look like. You may need to wait a moment until the fear subsides.

Or of course you could just reframe that fear – you could realise it's excitement in a Freddy Krueger costume. And anyway, the fear is based on the illusion of truth. Remember the benefit of alcohol was always an illusion. Alcohol has been dragging you down for years. You're not about to get dumped by a good-looking woman, you're running away from a psycho hose beast. You won't be pining for her, you'll be over the moon you managed to escape.

 Just think what your life would be like if alcohol wasn't holding you back?

Seriously, take a moment. Think about it, imagine it, picture the details. Reveal in it for a second. Good isn't it?

Captain casual

There are people who are quite happy as occasional drinkers. You're not one of those; if you were, you wouldn't be reading this book.

There are people who drink a safe amount; think 'great aunty who only ever drinks a small glass of sherry on Christmas day'. She drinks infrequently and the amount doesn't increase over time. That ain't you!

There are also people who'll tell you that they can "take it or leave it". But they're lying. Not to you, they're lying to themselves. Don't judge them, we've all been under-honest about our drinking at some point.

Can *you* be a genuinely happy casual drinker?

That's a question only you can answer. I can't because we've never met (unless we have met, in which case how are you? We should grab a coffee). But people who read books like this tend to have gone beyond the point where they can be happy with just the one drink every now and again.

There's a point that drinkers reach where they've drunk so much that they've fundamentally changed their brains. Their grey matter no longer reacts to alcohol the way a normal brain would. On a neurological level the difference is measurable.

That sounds bad. And it is. But only if you continue to put alcohol into your system. As soon as you stop, the fact that you react differently to alcohol won't matter, because you can't react to something that isn't in your body. On the flip side, the second you put alcohol into your body you'll revert to being an idiotic, booze-guzzling, happy slapper.

 The science is complex but the solution is clear.

Stop drinking. Forever.

Live the easy life

But leaving all that aside here's a simple fact: it's way easier not to drink. It is – bear with me here. If your brain is screaming "not drinking is harder than sitting through afternoon tea with your fiancé's parents when you really need to fart", don't worry. Just for now run with it.

Let's say that you're going out with a friend. It's Thursday. Old you would have drunk, probably a bit too much. What's new you going to do? If you're trying to be a happy casual drinker you have to answer the following questions:

- Do you drink tonight?
- If you're not drinking what do you tell your friends?
- How will you deal with the pressure they might put on you?
- If you do drink, how much do you drink?
- What do you drink?
- Do you leave after you have drunk your allowance?
- Do you stay and try to tough it out while hating drinking coke?
- What's the minimum amount you can drink and still justify eating a kebab?

It wouldn't be so bad if all you had to do was formulate a plan. Once you've gone through the mental gymnastics you must actually do what you planned.

Just for fun, ask yourself this question: how many times have you intended to drink a small amount and ended up drinking more than you meant to? A hundred times? A thousand times? A number that's so large it could be the GDP of a Pacific island nation?

You know that even a small amount of alcohol shreds your will-power and turns your judgement into mushy peas. After that first drink your brain is whistling and trying not to look guilty. If questioned it'll say "Plan? What plan?"

Being a casual drinker is hard work. But there's a solution.

Stop drinking. Forever.

At the moment you don't think you can do that. It's OK, I get it, but you must admit that if you were able to stop it would make life simpler, wouldn't it?

When you go out with a friend on Thursday, you don't drink. If they ask you why you're not drinking you say, "I don't drink". Simple.

And you never have to eat a kebab again. Unless you want to.

WHY REAL MEN QUIT

Do not cross

Psychologists call it a bright line. A clear mark in the sand which you don't cross. George Ainslie, renowned behavioural economist, borrowed the term from lawyers, but don't worry – it doesn't involve contracts written in blood.

Bright lines are clear, simple, unambiguous rules. The kind of rule that you have to notice yourself breaking because it's so black and white there can be no shades.

Effectively it's like drawing a line in your brain. On one side is all the stuff you don't do: drink alcohol, throw up on strangers, make a tit of yourself, eat fried chicken as a snack, or get confused between your girlfriend and her twin sister. On the other side is all the stuff you do, like live a fulfilling and successful life.

A lot of research has been done around bright lines and diets. It's notoriously difficult to get people to stick to a diet over the long term. Yet bright lines have been proven to help in follow up studies conducted over two years. If bright lines can help in something as complex as food choices it can help you with alcohol.

 Draw that line in the sand.

Now you get why this book is call *Real Men Quit*, rather than *Real Men Try to Limit their Intake, Do OK For a Bit, Then Fail, Get Miserable, Try Again, Fail Again, End Up Drinking More and Ultimately Go on to Live the Blurry Lives of Miserable Vagabonds Who Will Tell Anyone Who Will Listen How Much They Love the Booze.*

Stop drinking. Forever. Bang! Bright line.

More feeling?

Again, your brain may well be kicking into rebellion mode. It may be full of thoughts like "I can never stop, that's like asking Lee Mack to stop being funny". Just go with it for now and don't forget to breathe.

And seriously, how does that make you feel? This isn't the prelude to a session of Restorative Knitting, your reaction to the idea that

you'll never drink again is important. When we started, you probably had more fear than excitement. How does it feel now? OK, you might have had an initial rush of fear when you thought about never drinking again. But it'll stabilise.

Your fear-to-excitement ratio should be around fifty-fifty. That's a good place to be. If you feel you still have significant fear, ask yourself why that is. What are you afraid of? What do you think you're giving up? Is there something specific, like handling stress or socialising? You could go back and reread the chapters about them.

Or you could just grab the bull by the horns and shout "fear? What fear? This is just excitement dressed up as an 80s horror franchise that everyone except Duncan has forgotten."

Just don't panic. I'm about to explain why a part of you still has fear. But remember that we're trying to get to the point where you don't want to drink any more. If you can say "I want to stop drinking" and the only fear you feel comes from not knowing how to do it then you're golden, no matter how worried you might be.

Remember you're nearly there; you're nearly free. It's like you can almost see the sunlight glinting through the shadows. The life you want awaits. And it's going to be great.

 Imagine what you could do with more energy, less stress and more strength.

What a man you'll be.

" Down here it's made of wood & wire.

NICK CAVE

I was staring. Not in a rude way, not in the licentious, undressing her with my eyes style. I was vacant. Staring into the void that surrounds, the one we work so hard to ignore.

I had a cup of coffee; presumably I also had vague intentions of drinking it but at the moment my head was as empty as my bank account.

I heard the opening chords but they didn't really register.

"And now, the end is near..." Frank sang it like he was staring at the hangman's noose. I knew how he felt.

That was the point that I checked out of the coffee shop. Don't get me wrong, I love the song. I didn't leave physically, I disappeared even further into my head.

I was transported back a few years to a shabby evening in a sullied pub. I'd never quite understood why Jon loved places like that. I guess he thought they were real. I guess he liked the grime. I guess his pretension was the unpretentious.

"Can we leave yet?" I pleaded.

"Not till after the karaoke," he grinned. "I'll get another drink."

And that was pretty much that. He spent the evening holding court, I spent the evening holding my breath. It felt like several hours of being a heartbeat away from grievous bodily harm.

I don't know if the DJ sensed Jon could sing a bit or he just figured the song would be a good closer. Either way, he was right.

At five to eleven Jon was finally called to the mic. The immortal chords burst out of the half dead speakers but the people didn't care, they were getting what they wanted and, now, the end was near.

At least that was what they thought.

It was not a solo. It had a sing-a-long feel, like the crowd was singing 'My Way'. You could barely hear Jon, which was a shame as he really did have an impressive set of lungs, despite the smoking.

"And more, much more than this," the people sang and Jon accompanied.

"I did it my way," the crowd crooned. Jon just hung around until they started to run out of breath. One by one they faded, as the last one dropped away he stepped in and unleashed the full power of his voice.

It was his way.

They never managed to stay with him long enough. At the end of every chorus he left us in no doubt whose way it was.

But somehow it was still our way. It was all Jon's way but he let us share. There was no doubt who owned the song but we were all a part of it.

He owned the stage, he owned the evening, he owned the way.

And all I got was the guilt.

I let him live his way and where did that get him?

His way killed him. His way crumpled his pancreas in less than two decades. His way sapped his strength and broke him down. His way was the fast track to the darkness.

Guilt.

I should have sung louder. I should have overpowered his way. I should have nailed him down and made him behave differently. I should have done something.

Guilt.

What sort of a friend was I? I had let him down in the most basic way, violated the most basic commandment. I was not there for him. I didn't help. What sort of a human being, what sort of a man, was I?

Guilt.

I had failed him. I had failed our friends. I had failed his family. Worst of all I was slowly failing myself. Slowly walking the same way he walked. I was on the long, slow road to failure.

Guilt, nothing but dark, saturated guilt.

WHAT ALCOHOL DOES TO YOU

You don't need to ask your doctor to know that drinking is bad for you. You don't need your mum to tell you either. You don't need the government to tell you to drink responsibly. You know that alcohol is bad for you. You knew it from the very first sip. When that first drop of ethanol slides down your throat, you know it's poison.

Let's just dwell on that for a second. Your highly-tuned survival instincts tell you instantly that alcohol is toxic, yet you still drink it. You must have put a lot of effort into believing alcohol has benefits. After all, you're prepared to ignore what your body knows because you believe so strongly that alcohol will give you pleasure.

What you believe dictates what you do.

Why else do you think that religious nutjobs are prepared to blow themselves up to get into some sort of devotional Disneyland in the sky?

Beliefs matter.

You may even believe that red wine is good for you. True, you may only believe it in a vague way but if any part of your mind thinks that alcohol has health benefits, we need to stomp on that right now.

You may believe that science is divided. Personally, I favour the well designed, peer reviewed studies that conclusively demonstrate that alcohol has absolutely no health benefit, rather than the ones paid for by the alcohol industry.

Let me put it as fairly as possible: whilst very low levels of drinking *might* be correlated with *minor* health benefits, even moderate levels are *definitely* related to *major* health problems.

And you know this because you can't escape the fact that alcohol is a poison.

 In what other situation is poison good for you?

Alcohol is the only poison that's exempt from carrying hazardous chemicals warnings, which is a bit odd. If you read the *Daily Mail* – please don't, you'll go blind – you'd think we lived in a society obsessed with health and safety. Yet the most widely purchased poison doesn't have to carry any dangerous goods labels. Odd, right?

Weirdly, acetaldehyde must carry labels informing you how nasty it is. When you think about it, that's strange because acetaldehyde is what your body turns alcohol into. Here's what you'd expect to find on a bottle of acetaldehyde.

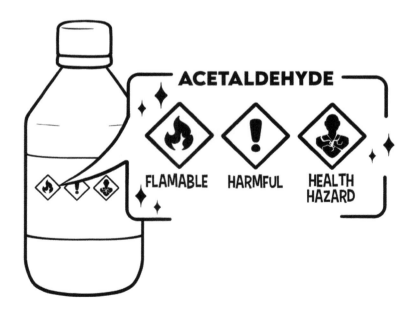

ACETALDEHYDE

FLAMABLE HARMFUL HEALTH HAZARD

Isn't it bizarre that alcohol is exempt from labelling laws but the stuff your body turns it into is subject to stringent hazardous chemical regulations?

People will believe anything

Part of you already knows that alcohol is poison. But for some reason you keep drinking it. You're probably thinking, "you already explained that Duncan. Trigger, Action, Celebration, Tracking, Bang!"

Yes, you managed to teach your brain that alcohol is actually a fun way of building friendships, reducing stress and generally being the man you always dreamed you would be. And that's a major part of your problem. Because now you're holding two opposing beliefs. Alcohol is poison: alcohol is brilliant.

Every time you drink, part of your brain is saying "hoorah, the nectar of the gods" and another part is going "Oh my god, not this again." How do you reconcile these two opposing reactions?

The short answer is that you never do but the long answer is way more interesting. It's called cognitive dissonance and even if you've never heard of it, you've been living it.

The truth is out there

Cognitive dissonance is the stress caused by holding two contradictory beliefs. It was named by a social psychologist called Leon Festinger who studied a small group called The Seekers. If we're feeling charitable, we could call them a group of people with non-traditional beliefs. Let's call them that; calling them alien apocalypse nutters isn't kind.

The group centred around a Chicago mystic with a penchant for automatic writing called Sister Thedra, real name Dorothy. Dorothy had received a message from Planet Clarion that said most of the world was going to be destroyed in a flood on December 21st, 1954. But don't panic, a flying saucer will rescue the true believers, whisking them off to a life of abundance in space.

What Festinger was interested in was what would happen when the flying saucer didn't arrive. For some reason he was pretty sure it wouldn't. Many people in the group had committed to the belief by selling their possessions and quitting their jobs – after all, you can't take it with you.

When the saucer didn't turn up they didn't all turn round and say "Oh well, we got that wrong, better phone the boss and start grovelling". Instead they came up with some elaborate stories that wove the absence of the flying saucer into the beliefs about the slightly less imminent destruction of the world.

The stories themselves don't matter. What's important is that their minds were presented with information which was contrary to what they believed and this created a sense of discomfort. That's the dissonance bit and cognitive means brain stuff.

They wanted to rid themselves of the brain pain. Surely the easiest way to do that would've been to say, "Oops, time to formulate a new world view"? But you know that people never do that. So they built a story that explained away the uncomfortable information. This allowed them to go on believing what they'd committed to. They created a comfortable illusion.

Sound familiar?

What do you believe?

A part of you knows that drinking is bad for you, that it causes more stress than it cures, that it makes you weak. But you've taught your mind to drink and you're going to keep rolling down that track until something changes the points and you set off in a new direction.

That's where the cognitive dissonance comes from. Those two opposing views; the "reasons to drink" and the "reasons not to drink". Here's a handy graphic that depicts it for you.

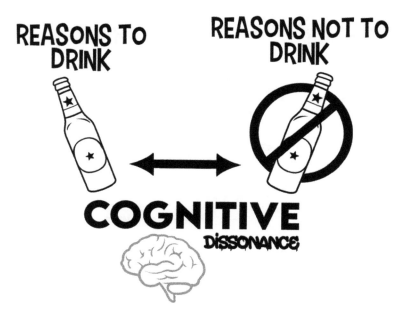

In essence, creating this mental discomfort is just another way that drinking causes stress. That isn't so bad until you consider the standard approach to getting people to stop drinking: tell them it's bad for them, it's ruining their health, it's jeopardising their relationships, and robbing them of their potential. Basically, increase the "reasons not to drink". That'll teach 'em. Except it never does, does it?

Big fat fear

Think back to the acetaldehyde warning label. Did it make you think "Ahh, I see now Duncan, alcohol is evil and it's time to completely reform my life"? Or did you think "Argghhhhhhhhhh!!! Somebody give me a goddamn drink"?

Look what happens when social pressure works on the "reasons not to drink".

If you increase the reasons not to drink without working on the reasons to drink, then all you've done is increase the brain pain. You've made the drinker feel uncomfortable. And what do drinkers do when they feel uncomfortable?

They drink.

In fact, it's worse than that because our minds are naturally disposed to focus on the positive and ignore the negatives. So the "reasons not to drink" part of our brain can be way bigger than the "reasons to drink" part of it, and we'll still give more weight to the much smaller "reasons to drink" part. Your brain will always maximise the pros and minimise the cons.

And that's why we're so keen to tell ourselves lies. We're just over the moon when we see adverts that show good looking people drinking. Deep in the recesses of our minds a little voice is saying, "I told you drinking was good – you're smarter than Elon Musk *and* you don't look like a waxwork sex offender". We create stories about how much fun drinking is. Actually, we don't need to create them, we pick them up fully formed from adverts, from films, from friends, from Amy Winehouse.

It wouldn't be so bad if we just kept it to ourselves. But we share, oh how we share! We'll tell anyone who'll listen how great alcohol is, how much fun we're having, how much we need that glass of wine after work. And we don't just mention it in conversation anymore, we post artfully framed shots of our drinks and moody black and white pics of our hangovers on Drinkstagram.

Worst of all, we try to block out the brain pain by getting completely trashed. We drunkenly grab hold of any old nonsense we can lay our hands on. We cling to the illusion that real men drink.

Do this instead

The trick is to remove the "reasons to drink". Then you're only left with the "reasons not to drink". And you're not far from that point. Given all the mental heavy lifting you've been doing you can see that alcohol has been taking you for a ride for years.

If you can see alcohol as it really is, if you can remove the illusion, then you'll be happy. You'll be free not just from alcohol but free from the cognitive dissonance that goes with it.

If you know that you're not missing out, if you *feel* it too, then you're there. Remember what Paul Tillich said: "without desire there is no temptation". He must have been smart because he was an existential theologian, and you have to be a proper egghead to figure out what an existential theologian even is.

 Once you don't want it, you stop wanting it.

And your desire for alcohol is fading. You're getting yourself free. Your life is about to change in so many ways. You'll be stronger and calmer, more energetic and happier. Man, you're going to love it.

WHAT ALCOHOL REALLY DOES TO YOU

Have you ever thought about what alcohol does to your brain? Probably not. If you have, you probably got no further than thinking about how it makes everything blurry, makes you fall over and stimulates the kebab cortex. Unsurprisingly, scientists have found that it does way more.

Your brain isn't stupid – in fact, it's amazing. It reacts quickly to restore balance because your brain loves balance. It doesn't like things off the straight and narrow, it likes homeostasis. Which is Greek for keeping stuff the same.

Your brain spends a lot of its time trying to keep you balanced. If you get too hot, it'll make you sweat. If you get too cold, it'll make you shiver. If you need calories, it'll tell you it's hungry. If you eat the entire cake, it'll make you feel sick. Balance.

Alcohol disrupts that balance. It causes your brain to release a powerful mix of chemicals. When you take that first sip it disturbs the equilibrium. It's like a seesaw; alcohol jumps onto one side and the seesaw swings in one direction.

But your brain doesn't like it, so it dumps a bunch of other chemicals into your head to counteract the alcohol. Forcing the seesaw to return to the middle, regaining its balance.

Which would be OK if that was as far as it went. But it's never that simple. The effects of the alcohol wear off but the effects of the reaction continue. Which is like the alcohol getting bored of the game, jumping off the seesaw and finding someone else to play with. That means the seesaw tips over to the other side with the wieght of the reaction.

You know all of this because you've heard of Isaac Newton. You know, "for every action, there is an equal and opposite reaction." What comes up must go down.

B follows A like down follows up

Newton is a bit theoretical. How does it work out when you're drinking on a Friday night? Let's think of it as two separate processes. The alcohol enters your system and starts a little brain chemical party – let's call that the A process. Your body reacts to this massive wave of stimulation with an opposite set of chemicals. Let's call that the B process.

A process is "up", B process is "down". As high as the A process goes, there will be an equally sized B process. When you start drinking after work on Friday you'll feel the A process until you go to bed. You'll start to feel the effects of the B process when you wake up on Saturday morning.

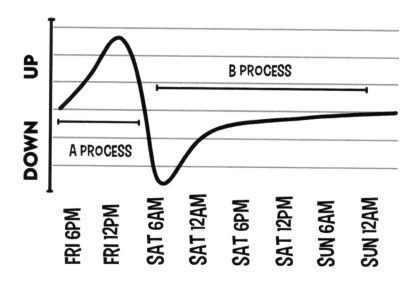

The effects of the B process are relatively mild. You feel lethargic, you feel negative, you feel more sensitive to pain. In short you don't feel like you're dying but you also don't feel like yourself. You don't notice it because you're good at ignoring it but trust me, it's knocking you off your game.

If you wonder why I'm calling them the A process and B process, it's because that's what the scientists who came up with the opponent-processes theory call it. I know, I know, A process, B process, it's dull. But scientists have no imagination. If they could weave the mental unreality, then we'd all be using hoverboards by now.

Hangxiety

Let me make one thing completely clear: I'm not talking about hangovers. I'm not talking about the big head. If that was going to put you off you wouldn't drink.

The B process is much more subtle. No one ever talks about it. But you're starting to understand what's going on – you're starting to face up to the real effects of alcohol. You're increasing those "reasons not to drink", and that increases your cognitive dissonance. Are you tempted to ignore it?

Of course you are! That's why most people haven't heard of the opponent-processes theory. Anyone who drinks finds it too uncomfortable to talk about.

If they did, they'd have to pretend the suffering was special, like they pretend that a hangover is a badge of honour. But social media will never manage to rebrand the opponent-processes theory because it'll change the way you see alcohol.

You cannot cheat the B process, no matter what you do. It is impervious to milk before going out, bacon sandwiches, or the echinacea your hippy-chick ex used to swear by.

You will suffer from the B process. It's as inevitable as death, taxes and your boss making a stupid decision.

 You can't fight your body's attempt to achieve balance.

Must come down

We've seen the effect of a couple of drinks on Friday. But let's face it, no one ever just drinks on Friday. By Saturday evening the B process is either mild enough to ignore or it's been gnawing away at you so much you're shouting, "Give me a goddamn drink!". Either way you're opening a bottle on Saturday too. And Sunday – why not, it's the weekend.

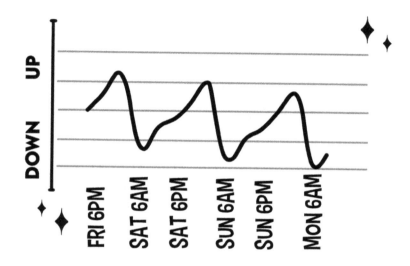

When you drink on Friday you start from "normal" and the A process takes you up. On Saturday morning you feel the B process. But when you start drinking on Saturday you're still in the B process – you go up but not as far. On Sunday you start from even further down. This time the A process only just takes you past normal.

Incidentally, a small glance at where you are on Monday morning might explain why you don't like the start of the week. You could have the most engaging job and a non-idiotic boss and you still wouldn't be happy getting up because you're fighting three days' worth of B process.

How low can you go?

I want to take this opportunity to reiterate that these graphs do not depict hangovers. They show your body's attempt to rebalance. You get an A process and a B process every time you drink, whether or not you get a hangover. In fact, it doesn't even matter if you get drunk or not. A process: B process. Day: Night.

You cannot fight it. If you drink any alcohol the B process will follow the A process. It has happened every time you've ever drunk. The chances are, if you noticed the B process, you explained it away: I'm not a morning person, I didn't sleep well, my god this job is stressful.

Here's a novel thought – maybe you are a morning person? Maybe you've been convinced you don't do mornings for the last twenty years because of your alcohol intake rather than your biological make up?

You cannot fight the process. There's always a reaction to every action – which may be the only useful thing you ever learnt in science.

It's an inevitable biological process that exposes alcohol's illusion of truth. It doesn't help you handle stress, it is stress. It doesn't soothe your nerves, it causes them. It doesn't make you strong, it's liquid weakness.

You know it doesn't work. In fact, because you have awesome taste, you probably have "I fought the law and the law won" spinning around your head. Breakin' rocks in the hot sun...

It's worse than that

Of course, if you keep doing this to yourself for long enough then your brain will eventually wise up. It won't just react by pumping chemicals into your system, it starts to make sure the ones that alcohol stimulates become less effective.

It's called down regulation. It's subtle but it's one of the worst aspects of drinking. It's like your brain sticks a big block at the bottom of the seesaw to make sure that alcohol can no longer disturb the balance.

Alcohol is jumping up and down on the seesaw but it isn't moving. Booze isn't having much fun.

The tragedy is that alcohol uses the same system as a lot of important stuff. It uses the system that you use for happiness, for enjoying everything from food to sex to proving your boss is wrong and shouting, "In your face, space coyote!".

Think about that for a second. If you drink alcohol for any length of time then, to protect itself, your brain will reduce your enjoyment of life. Alcohol robs you of joy, excitement and victory. It takes your 4K, HDR, Dolby Vision life and turns it into a grainy, black and white cathode ray ordeal.

 Alcohol affects you even when you aren't drinking.

By drinking you're reducing your brain's ability to enjoy life, learn new stuff, your chance to become a better human being. You can't fight the B process, it's too strong. The good news is you can fight alcohol. Better yet, it's weak.

Is it pain or is it displeasure?

I don't tell you all of this to try to make you think, "wow, booze's so bad for me". What I want you to realise is that booze does nothing for you.

You knew alcohol had negative consequences before you started reading. What you need to understand is that what you perceive as the positive benefits of alcohol is the removal of the negative consequences that alcohol caused in the first place.

In other words, the benefit of drinking is that it removes the pain it causes.

It's not always easy to get. Let's think about it like this: if I came round your house and started to blast One Direction's greatest hits at full volume you'd quickly get annoyed. You'd feel better when the police came and moved me on, but you'd feel better because you had returned to normal, not because you'd improved.

Drink for long enough and alcohol stops giving you a boost, it just turns off the One Direction album in your head and returns you to where you should be. The A process stops being an up, because all it does is remove the discomfort of the B process.

There are two valuable lessons here. One, there is no pleasure in drinking. Two, it's best not to give me your address.

" There must be some way out of here, said the joker to the thief.

BOB DYLAN

I awoke in the dark, in the cold, on a rock slick with mud. Where in Hull was I? I saw nothing. I worried that I had blinded myself with vodka but I remembered that I didn't live on a Soviet collective farm, so it seemed unlikely.

Unfortunately, I could feel. And I felt bad. No, scratch that – I felt stinking, crying out, bury me in toxic waste bad. I could smell too and I could smell damp and somewhere, far off, I could hear running water.

Dark? Damp? Brass monkey cold? An idea starts to penetrate the thickness of my head. I must have pitched up in the cave of alcohol-induced misery, the fabled Cavern of the Crapulous Hangoria. And I had a gnawing sense of déjà vu.

A rasping noise. A flare of light.

My abused eyes began to focus, and I realised that someone had struck a match. As my irises stopped down a few notches I made out a humanoid figure lighting a cigarette.

"Help," I croaked through my wooden mouth.

Finally, my eyes adjusted and I saw.

"Hank?" For all the world he resembled a shaggy-cheeked, arse-scratching troll that wouldn't have looked out of place in the hall of the Mountain King.

The match fizzed out.

"You have to help, my soul is out of joint. I think I've dislocated a cortex?" I pleaded through the after-effects.

He took a long drag but didn't reply.

I pushed myself up to look around. My eyes had adjusted but it was too dark to make much out. How I got here was a complete blank. There were flashes, a bottle of Chartreuse, the opening chord from a song I couldn't name and something about an ostrich and a kebab shop.

The way in was a mystery. The way out? I had about a 1 in 360 degree chance of finding the exit.

"What is..." said Hank, his voice resonant with pseudo-profundity, "...the difference between a troll and a man?".

"There must be some way out of here."

"What is..." repeated Hank in his intellectual voice.

"OK. OK." I replied, "what is the difference between a troll and a man?"

Hank puffed himself up like a low-rent bodhisattva.

"They both live in darkness. But man brews the potion to convince himself there is light in the gloom."

Hank revealed a nouveau canister of otherworldly liquid, a pewter medallion hanging from its neck with the words "drink me" inscribed in a Tolkienian script.

"You don't fool me Hank, I've lived in the light my whole life. I'm not prepared to believe we're living in some folklore matrix. I've seen the sun."

Hank shot me an uncanny look and launched into: "Only a modicum of methodological scepticism is required to appreciate that sensation as a mode of perception is, at best, obscure and confused."

"What?"

"You can't believe your eyes, you can only trust what you drink."

"Can't we just leave?"

He shrugged.

I mustered my remaining cognitive battalions in an attempt to think this through. Hank raised his flask with a mischievous flourish.

"Behold the vodka of life, the path to seeing light in the darkness."

Just my luck. Not only do I get stranded in a cave but I have to put up with an epistemologically-challenged hobgoblin.

"Come on Hank, you must know which way is out."

He crossed his arms and pointed in both directions.

"Fine, I'll drink the elixir of folk-wittery."

I took a slug from the flask. It elbowed its way down my throat like an old friend in an acid overcoat. The world vacillated on a declining balance.

I squinted. Maybe there was a light in the distance.

HOW YOUR MIND WORKS

The question people often ask me, other than why are you standing on my lawn playing One Direction, is how does my mind work? And I say, "your brain is like a mushy grey banana split; there are two parts and it has a cherry on top." These aren't physical parts and the cherry was an exaggeration. These parts are systems and psychologists call them System 1 and System 2. What did I tell you about scientists? Literally no creativity. Man, we could be living on the moon by now.

System 1 is the part of your brain that does things automatically and System 2 is the bit that can do some real thinking.

The thinking bit is far smarter. It's capable of reason, logic and might even manage to solve a fiendish sudoku puzzle. But it's lazy. It likes to leave stuff up to the other bit because the other bit doesn't get tired and want to have a lie down.

Putting on your watch is a good example of the automatic bit. It's so easy you don't give it a second thought, pure System 1. So easy it's automatic, you could even do it hungover – in fact, you probably have.

To understand what the thinking bit does, try putting your watch on the wrong wrist. It'll be far from automatic; you're going to have to mentally wrestle it. You'll be far more aware of what you're doing and you probably couldn't do it hungover. Not because you really couldn't, but it would be hard enough to make the lazy bit say, "sod it, I don't need a watch today".

To save you the effort of trying to remember the difference between system 1 and system 2 I'm going to make an analogy. The automatic bit is sort of like a computer so I'm going to call it The Terminator. Which means that the bit that does the thinking must be called John Connor. Hasta la vista, baby.

Who is Hank

If you've been paying attention to the story bits in this book you'll be under the impression that I have a friend called Hank. He's not real.

Not in the sense of artistic licence, like I made him up so I didn't have to blame Andy (it's all his fault by the way). No, he isn't a real fleshy, tangible human. He's a voice in my head that tells me to drink wine, eat pizza and spend the day watching snooker.

Hank is my inner Terminator.

Admittedly, he's a bargain-basement Terminator, more tin foil than titanium. But he's still relentless. He's that automatic process that kept me drinking for all those years. Hank lives in the deep, dank regions of my head. He's always ready to remind me that I deserve a drink, no thought required. He's as automatic as my wife being five minutes late for everything.

I'm not saying that I have dissociative identity disorder, I don't think there's a little metal homunculus camped out in my brain. Hank's partly a metaphor for the way different parts of our brains interact but in a sense he's real. He's that little voice that's so quick to come up with a seemingly good reason why I should have a drink.

 Hank is the automation in my head.

The thing is, you have a little Terminator inside you too. If you're quiet for a moment or two you may well hear him talking. He's that voice that is saying "stop reading, open a bottle, you've had a hard day, poor you, you should relax, you deserve a drink". Sounds familiar?

That's your Terminator. That's the automatic bit of your brain. It's a part of you but it's not all of you.

The biggest part of you is John Connor. The better part of you is the bit that does the thinking. The bit that's going to save the human race.

Having realised that your inner Terminator has been ruining your life might make you want to punch him in the face. Don't, you'll break your hand. Think about it; what would John Connor do?

Just in case you haven't watched the films for a while, or you have no idea who John Connor is, let me tell you. He'd reprogramme The Terminator. He'd turn it into an ally.

How to reprogramme a Terminator

I'm not saying your brain's actually a robot from the future. It's not. In fact, it's not even a computer. What I'm saying is there's a bit of it that you can code like a computer. The good news is you don't need even the slightest clue what </p=$!*> means.

Even calling it If/Then coding is over-spicing the guacamole. If/Then coding is simply the idea that, If: A happens, Then: do B. For example, If: strange man says he has puppies, Then: run like billy-oh.

Let's look at how that relates to drinking.

To start with there's a trigger – for argument's sake a party. At first, when you're exposed to the trigger, the human bit has to have a think. Let's imagine it goes like this: "Oh, there's alcohol, we like alcohol, why don't we drink some?" You have a drink and you celebrate. Trigger. Action. Celebration. Bother! Accidental change.

As you also know, the more you go down the accidental pathway, the stronger the tracking, the more attention your brain pays to alcohol. You become subconsciously more aware of the triggers. That's the attention loop. And that means the action becomes automatic, the

action becomes a piece of If/Then coding. The Terminator has acquired a target.

I'll be back

The next time you go to a party and see the trigger you don't need to think about it. You no longer need the human bit. You've created a piece of If/Then coding. If: party. Then: beer. Easy.

You see the trigger, The Terminator interprets it as an If. There follows the appropriate Then. The If/Then code has been fulfilled. The Terminator terminates. The beer is in your hand, no conscious thought required, John Connor can hang out at the BMX park with his buddies, no human involvement needed.

Worse than that, you start to associate more and more things with alcohol. If: stress, Then: alcohol. If: dinner, Then: alcohol. If: friends, Then: alcohol. If: holiday, Then: alcohol. Taken to its logical conclusion:

 If: awake, Then: alcohol.

Your own personal Terminator

The Terminator, the automation, is an important survival mechanism. Look at it this way – what would happen if you had to have a little internal discussion when you saw a car coming towards you? If: car, Then: get out of way. Survival of the best programmed.

You know that little automated voice, the one that whispers, "drink the wine", "drink the beer", "drink whatever you can lay your filthy hands on". You also know that if you don't lay your filthy hands on some booze sooner or later then that little voice is going to get annoyed.

That's partly why drinking alcohol seems to give you a sense of relief. You'd be forgiven for thinking that it's a good thing. But it's not actual relief. What you've done is calmed down Hank. And once he's calm he stops pestering you to give him a drink.

Honestly, if you had a miniscule Terminator running around your head, hell-bent on getting a drink, it would be uncomfortable. You can see that, right?

We're back to me standing on your lawn playing One Direction – what you enjoy about having a drink is not that it brings you comfort, it's that it ends discomfort.

 The benefit of drinking is that it removes the pain it causes.

The distinction is subtle and hard to feel because pleasure and pain use the same part of our brain. But it's important.

To take it one step further, why does Hank shut up when you give him a drink? He only wants a drink because you've taught him to want a drink. So giving him a drink isn't going to end the discomfort, it's not going to change his desire for a drink. It's only going to reinforce what he's already learnt.

Let's face it, getting a Terminator to stop chasing you is good but not having a Terminator chasing you in the first place is better.

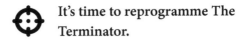 **It's time to reprogramme The Terminator.**

Best of all, it won't involve time travel.

From persecutor to protector

Let's just overemphasise the point: Hank's The Terminator; you're John Connor. And while Hank's relentless, he has one key vulnerability. He does what he's programmed to do.

You can write new If/Then coding for Hank. You can change The Terminator from enemy to ally.

Understanding how The Terminator and John Connor interact is a part of what's going to get you out of the mess. But before we get too deeply into that you need to acknowledge that you're capable of changing the way you think. You need to be confident in your reprogramming abilities before you start messing with Arnie's internal wiring. Let's look at an example of when you've changed.

Making the first cup of coffee of the day is something you don't need to think about. It's pure Terminator – If: awake, Then: coffee. The If, or trigger, will vary depending on your morning routine. For me it comes while I'm getting my daughter's breakfast. She's reliable, she wants breakfast every day. Actually, first she wants a hug, then food. That's when The Terminator jumps in. If: making daughter's breakfast, Then: make coffee. Trigger and action powered by If/Then coding. While my daughter's happily munching away, I'm smelling that caffeinated aroma, the celebration follows.

It's all automatic. Everything runs in the background like a Skynet caffeination system.

But it doesn't have to be. With a bit of conscious effort, I could change the coding. I could take any If and add any Then. That's reprogramming The Terminator.

Learning to shout

Let's just say I wanted to start shouting "Real Men Quit" in the morning. I could take my If – operating the Nespresso machine – and add a Then. Initially, it would require some effort from the human bit to remember – If: coffee machine, Then: "Real Men Quit". But the more I did it the less it would be a human activity, the more it would become something my personal Terminator would take care of.

The tracking would kick in and The Terminator would already be looking out for the If. The tracking reinforces the coding. If: coffee. Then: shout. If: shout. Then: celebrate.

But we're not really talking about me, we're really talking about you. You've changed your brain. In about the amount of time it's taken to read 26 chapters you've reprogrammed The Terminator.

 You've reformed your mind by creating a new If/Then code, and that's amazing.

Just in case you've forgotten how doors work: the way in is the way out. By changing your mind, you're changing your life. So keep shouting "Real Men Quit" every morning and celebrate like no one's looking.

And it's like your mum says – that's Sarah Connor, not your actual mum – "Because if a machine, a Terminator, can learn the value of human life, maybe we can, too."

What you have to realise is that your life used to be *The Terminator*. The Terminator was trying to destroy you. But now it's *Terminator 2: Judgement Day*; the explosions are bigger, the stunts are ridiculous, and The Terminator is going to save you.

" Ooh, let me get it back, let me get it back, let me get it back, baby, where I come from.

BONHAM, JONES, PAGE & PLANT

Clunk. God I love this machine; putting the pods in reminds me of a breech-loading rifle. I drifted into my head as my man-toy worked on my man-coffee.

Coffee.

Beans make coffee. Beans make chocolate. Chocolate coats coffee beans. Chocolate coated coffee beans. And Jon.

Who ate an entire packet of them in soupçon short of twenty minutes.

We laughed so much. The memories of that afternoon come through a smudgy filter because my eyes were not dry for hours.

What started the merriment was soon forgotten. Soon, it was just his face that was funny. He'd try to stop giggling, try to pull his features into an arrangement of a serious nature. He'd fail. He'd laugh. I'd laugh. He'd laugh again. I'd laugh again. We set aside the trappings of adulthood for the innocent glee of children, hilarity that goes on and on until it hurts but you still don't want to stop. Laughter, pain, laughter, pain, laughter. But still, you don't ever want it to stop.

Why did it have to stop?

The coffee was ready but I was not. I was lost, not in the memory, not in the regret.

In what exactly?

I lack the vocabulary to describe the weight that I felt. It wasn't a pain, more emotional ballast, a sorrowfully sunk feeling, a slippery melancholy over the injustice of it all. Maybe. A wistful desire to have him back.

Please, someone, bring him back.

I glanced down at the cup, I'd swap that sleek, black brew for just one of his esoteric jokes. I'd swap every coffee I'll ever drink for just one more laugh. There are few prices I wouldn't pay for another afternoon of squawking, iconoclastic tomfoolery.

Please, just a little more Jon.

YOUR WHEELS ARE SPINNING

I know you've drunk alcohol so I know you know how it works but let's just clarify. Your personal Terminator says "let's have a drink." Assuming that you're not driving a car at the time, the other part of your brain, aka John Connor, doesn't even get involved. You drink. You feel bad.

Maybe you're pushing back. Maybe you're thinking I don't feel bad when I'm drinking – quite the opposite. Granted you probably feel better when you take that first sip. But that's just because The Terminator wanted a drink and you've given him one. When you do that he shuts up and the uncomfortable feeling of wanting a drink goes away.

Congratulations, you've just muted One Direction's greatest hits, temporarily.

That feeling of wanting a drink is a nervous, anxious, empty feeling. You're probably not aware of it as you drink every time The Terminator tells you to. If you really want to experience it go to the pub, drink orange juice. The irritation of expecting alcohol and not getting it will come soon enough.

Keep on running

That uncomfortable feeling is part of the system that creates the tracking. I call it the Running Wheel of Dopamine Hell. Now you're going to take one look at the illustration and say, "Dude, that's a hamster wheel". I see where you're coming from, but running wheel is correct. The science-types use rats. They don't use hamsters because hamsters are too cute. The ethics board won't approve getting hamsters drunk. So it's a running wheel.

And you probably thought the wheels were just somewhere for the rats to exercise. But running on a wheel isn't like running. Lab rats use their wheels way more than they need to, so much so that their tails permanently change shape to match the curve of the wheel.

Running and running wheels differ in excitement levels just like lying down and lying down between two oiled-up Amazonian warrior-women differs. In fact, running wheels are so much fun that scientists believe they activate the same dopamine pathway as, well, oiled-up Amazonians. No doubt about it – Running Wheel of Dopamine Hell.

Drinking wheel

Scientists would refer to having a drink as a stimulus but I'm going to use the more complex technical term "beer". When you drink the "beer" it releases dopamine which creates a sense of comfort.

By comfort I mean the absence of pain. This shouldn't be mistaken for pleasure. As the dopamine decreases then the comfort is replaced with discomfort. If you have another drink the discomfort is replaced with comfort. You usually go on doing this all the way till sleep, avoiding the discomfort till morning.

But the discomfort is there. And it creates the tracking, the desire to repeat the "beer", the desire to remove the discomfort and regain the comfort.

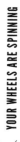

DOPAMINE UP

DOPAMINE HELL

COMFORT

DISCOMFORT

DOPAMINE DOWN

Just to make it crystal clear, I'm using the word comfort in a particular way. I don't mean comfort as in duvets and sleeping till noon, I'm talking about comfort as in *not* having your back, sack and crack waxed while listening to Michael Bublé.

When you give in to Hank and have a drink you feel comfortable; you feel better than you did before.

> It's not the alcohol that you enjoy, it's ending the discomfort of wanting it.

Shutting up Hank is the comfort. And it's pretty thin comfort because it's inevitably followed by discomfort. The comfort you get from the dopamine must be followed by the discomfort you get as it starts to leave. Up: Down. A process: B process.

Isn't there a problem?

But aren't we using this system to learn not to drink? Aren't we just going to make ourselves miserable by creating discomfort? Absolutely not! We're using the Ferris Wheel of Dopamine Heaven. Totally different. It might sound like the Running Wheel of Dopamine Hell but there's a massive difference. Let me explain.

The level of dopamine in your brain naturally fluctuates for all sorts of sciencey reasons. Some things make those levels increase normally – things like doing a good job, eating real food and an oiled-up Amazonian. Then other things cause crazy increases, like hardcore drugs, hardcore porn or hardcore junk food. It's the difference between strawberries and strawberry daiquiri.

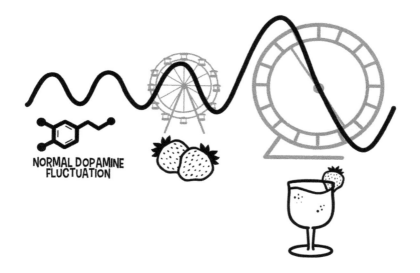

NORMAL DOPAMINE
FLUCTUATION

If you think about it, this is a bit odd as Ferris wheels are massive – they even call them big wheels – and running wheels are small. Yet the effect on your brain is the other way around. Weird, hey?

It's the difference between eating a punnet of strawberries and a pound of refined sugar. Eating strawberries makes you feel good. It raises your dopamine levels in a normal way. It creates the tracking: if you see some strawberries you'll eat them because they're good. Normal brain stuff.

Strawberries cause the release of dopamine and, when it hits those receptors, it creates pleasure. Because there's no strawberry-related discomfort to remove, you enjoy it. The tracking comes from a desire to repeat the pleasurable experience rather than to remove the discomfort.

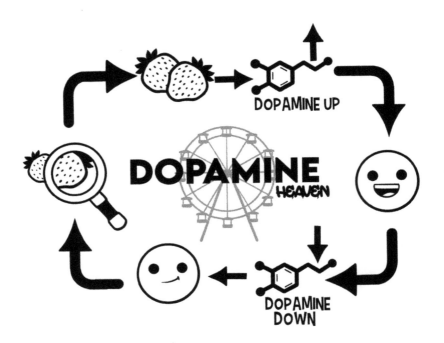

Strawberries feel different

In one respect, there shouldn't be any difference when you eat a pound of refined sugar – after all, the active ingredients of sugar and strawberries only differ by the odd CH_2OH molecule. And what's a CH_2OH molecule between friends?

But that's a reductionist way of thinking. It makes a huge difference. Your body processes the two things differently and, unlike the strawberries, refined sugar creates a shock and awe dopamine airstrike. That's why kids go bat-shit crazy on Haribo in a way they don't with strawberries.

It's the difference between a small spike which returns to normal and a massive spike which must drop to discomfort. It's the difference

between tracking something you get enjoyment from and tracking something that stops you hurting.

 It's the difference between getting pleasure and ending pain.

The Tactical Change System uses your brain's normal chemical circuits at a normal chemical level. It rides the Ferris Wheel of Dopamine Heaven. Alcohol, on the other hand, uses the same system but not in the same way – it's using the Running Wheel of Dopamine Hell. So don't worry, using dopamine to learn not to drink won't make you miserable. Quite the opposite. It's using your brain the way it's meant to be used.

After the first sip

Once you've had your first couple of slugs of booze and the dopamine is flooding your brain you reach that initial point of comfort. After that you're just drinking. Pouring the stuff down your throat entirely without thinking about it. You aren't even aware you're doing it. It's automatic killer cyborg. It's not you that's drinking, it's Hank. That means you can't be enjoying it. If you aren't aware that you're doing it, if it's automatic, then you can't enjoy it.

Any enjoyment comes from what you're doing; socialising, relaxing, getting double-teamed by oil-covered warrior women. You enjoy the situation, not the alcohol. Honestly, when was the last time you sat in a darkened room with nothing to distract you so you could revel in the pure enjoyment of a drink? You've never done that because pouring alcohol down your throat isn't enjoyable.

 Alcohol on its own is no fun.

If you don't believe me, try it. This evening go into an empty room with a few bottles of whatever takes your fancy. Turn the lights right down – don't make it pitch black or you'll probably break your bloody neck. Then get drunk. See how much fun it is. And no cheating

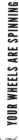

– leave your phone in the other room. And don't even think about watching sports. This is just you, the booze and nothing else.

And while you're at it you'll be forced to truly experience the effects of alcohol. You'll be forced to notice the relief you get when you end the dissatisfied state of wanting a drink, when you turn off One Direction.

You won't be able to miss the unpleasant sensations that you've learnt to ignore: the blurring of your senses and the slight dizziness, the nausea and the unpleasant changes in your internal temperature – all this awaits you. You'll notice that the physical sensations of being drunk aren't particularly pleasant.

I expect you'll also get phenomenally bored. Drinking is boring. It's your friends, or football, or horny fighting females, that are interesting.

I AM NOT YOUR DRILL INSTRUCTOR

Shouting at people isn't my style. I'd rather help you see things differently, in a gentle and humorous way. But sometimes people need a jolt. Sometimes they need a drill instructor.

I've been lucky that in the last few years I have met some really amazing people who've helped me to identify and examine the beliefs that were holding me back. But there have also been times when I just needed a kick up the arse.

Think for a moment about the idea that alcohol helps you through the bad times. Do you still think that's true?

Most of the head-junk you had about alcohol has been blown to kingdom come. But when you really push men, they often fall back on the idea that alcohol numbs their pain. That it provides them with some value because it distracts them from their problems.

That's why, like me, they sometimes need a boot to the backside.

They get the rest of it, they see it doesn't help them deal with their problems, but they still think they enjoy a little respite from their troubles.

Yet, if we add up the stuff you know – the dopamine discomfort, the cognitive dissonance and the B process – you can see how alcohol is clearly making your problems harder to deal with. And that's ignoring the stuff we haven't mentioned, like alcohol's effect on GABA.

GABA, or gamma-aminobutyric acid, is a brain chemical that helps you chill out, rather than a crap 70s cover band.

Alcohol starts off by increasing GABA and reducing your anxiety. But you know that means it'll be going in the other direction to compensate. GABA has its downswing just like the B process. You wake up the next day with less GABA floating about and you're drowning in anxiety.

And don't forget that if you drink for any length of time your brain will respond by reducing the release of GABA which will make you more anxious overall. Alcohol doesn't just give you more problems than it solves, it makes you scared to face them.

Do you want less stress?

The good news is you'll always have problems. If you think about it, you don't want fewer problems – life is made up of problems. Your family causes you problems. Your friends cause you problems. Your work causes you problems. Your health causes you problems. You can't live a fulfilling life and *not* have problems.

 A life without problems is a life without life.

My daughter is a great example. If someone took her away then my life would suddenly become enormously stressful. Yet having her around is also pretty stressful – when will she learn not to lick lampposts?

You're stuck with a stressful job, stressful friends and a stressful family. But if you sacked them all off and lived in a cave you'd have the stress of missing them. And living in a cave is fraught with problems, like how on earth do you get Netflix in a cave?

Stop craving less problems!

You don't want a stress-free life. You don't want less problems. You want better solutions. And what's the worst solution you can think of?

Alcohol.

Do this!

If you still cling to the idea that there's some value in trying to hide from your problems then I want to introduce you to Kevin McDonnell, serial entrepreneur, peddler of colourful language and the kind of guy that just won't let you hide.

You know what he'd say to you? Get out of your own way.

In fact, he'd say it with a tad more profanity, but that would be the nub of it. Your problems aren't going anywhere so stop hiding and do something.

Do. Something.

Doing almost anything is better than doing nothing.

He'd also say that at times like these you don't need a friend. You don't need someone to say, "There, there, it's OK, have another drink and ignore the shouty Irish guy." You don't need excuses, you need someone to call you out on your bullshit.

Whinging and moaning about stress is bullshit.

Drinking is bullshit.

Thinking that someone or something else is stopping you is bullshit.

 GET OUT OF YOUR OWN WAY!!!

Setting the bar high

Kevin forced me to take ownership, to stop thinking about the things I can't change and start grinding away at the things I can. Other than that, what I like about him is that he expects so much from me. And, in that spirit, I'm expecting a lot from you.

I don't just expect you to quit. I don't just expect you to reaffirm your status as a real man. I don't just expect you to start living your best life.

 I expect you to smash the shit out of it.

Maybe your journey will end up like Kevin's, from debt to multiple business success. Maybe it'll be like mine, from wannabe writer to four-times published bestseller. Or maybe it'll be something totally different. Just remember, I expect it to be spectacular.

I expect you to go from ignoring your problems to standing in front of them in the fullness of your manpower. I expect you to *own* your life. I expect you to burn like an inferno, crush it like a monster truck and dance like Nataraja.

Get out of your own way and get on with it.

" We are all just prisoners here, of our own device.

FELDER, HENLEY AND FREY

It's not that I don't like people, I do. I'd happily talk to a solid 98% of people, anyone but psychopaths and hedge fund managers.

It was just that I didn't want to talk to anyone at that moment. I'd pulled a twelve-hour shift and that meant twelve hours of enforced jollity. I just wanted to be alone.

It was, therefore, a bad idea to get onto a bus. It might've worked if I could sit alone, if no one occupied the seat next to me, if I didn't have to share.

And that was a game I could play. Scowling was key; reading helped. If you're not staring at your phone then you're probably a se-rial killer...

Scowl.

Read.

Scowl.

"Do you mind if I sit down?" All was lost. I had failed. Sharing.

Mind you, she looks old. Maybe she's only going a couple of stops.

"Help yourself," I replied.

"Oh good, I wouldn't want to stand the whole way to Abingdon," she said cheerfully.

Damn, she was going to the end of the line.

"Town is so busy today."

Worse than having to share my seat – apparently I had to share my thoughts too. I dog-eared my page and placed the book in my bag.

"I suppose so," I said wearily.

"What's the matter deary? You sound like you've got the weight of the world on your shoulders."

"Chalk it up to a hard day, or a hard week, or a hard month, or just call it a hard year."

"What you need is to read that book of yours..."

I raised an eyebrow.

"...in a nice long bath, make it as hot as you can manage."

"I've got to go to the pub with a friend."

"Nonsense, a grubby old pub won't help you relax, you need a good long soak."

"I don't think Hank will see it like that."

"Hank will understand."

I snorted a laugh, "He's pretty insistent."

"Well then, he can't be much of a friend can he?"

"He gets whiney. He'll moan all evening if I don't go for a drink."

She looked sternly at me; I got the distinct impression that I had let her down.

I opened my mouth but the response died before it had formed.

"Real men help. They support their friends, they care." She crossed her arms like a century-old dragon who's just had her hoard fiddled with.

Yet...

Maybe she was right. I thought that Hank was my friend, that he was looking out for me. But was he?

That question nagged, maybe...

Maybe his actions weren't those of a friend. Maybe he wasn't giving me what I needed. Maybe he was only interested in what he could get. He was selfish.

Now I'd challenged my beliefs about alcohol, now I'd seen it for what it was, his selfishness was glaring. I couldn't understand how I never noticed it before.

It all crunched into place, like I'd reversed into a bollard. Hank wasn't helping me. He wasn't giving me what I needed: he was only interested in what he could get. He'd never helped me. He pretended it was all for my benefit but really it was always about him.

I looked up.

And there it was, a bright red button. "Stop" inscribed upon it in large friendly letters. Stop? My finger hovered over it, could I do it? Should I do it? Wasn't this what I needed?

I pressed.

"Thanks." I yelled at the lady as I grabbed my bag and tore down the stairs.

The bus had hardly stopped when I jumped off. I took a huge gulp of air. A sense of peace came over me. I'd done it. This was it. I looked around as the blur of my excitement dissipated.

Hey, this isn't my stop!

As the bus pulled off, I realised I had a mile and a half to walk.

I smiled. I guess the wheels on the bus really do go round and round.

It did not matter. I'd spent too long waiting for my stop. I was certain it didn't matter where you got off the bus, how you got off the bus, the only thing that mattered was getting off the bus.

I set off down the road. It was different, a far cry from how it had seemed yesterday. All of a sudden I was a stranger in a strange life.

THE DOOR MARKED EXIT

We've reached the point where you have to make a decision. It's make your mind up time. And you have three options:

KEEP DRINKING.

CUT BACK.

QUIT.

If doing nothing was going to work then you'd be doing nothing, yet you're not. You're reading this book. Doing nothing is a no go.

You can try to moderate your drinking. There are people out there who advocate this. I'm not one of them. Personally, I think that if you have got to the point where you've acknowledged that drinking is an issue, then you've passed the point that moderate drinking is a viable option.

You may think, "yes, but Duncan, can't I use the Tactical Change System to control my drinking?" It sounds tempting but it won't work. The Tactical Change System is a way of changing your behaviour by managing your thoughts. Managing your thoughts takes conscious effort. That's the attention bit of the attention loop: you have to pay attention to create the loop.

It's not hard but it takes mental effort. And what happens when you drink? The bit of your brain used for effort takes a little holiday.

Don't drink and think

I learnt this the hard way. I was working with someone who, despite having a Nobel-level intellect, had still managed to get trapped on the alcohol rollercoaster. Due to his history he couldn't stop cold, so we did a managed detox. We reduced the amount that he drank every day for about ten days.

While we're here let me point out that most drinkers can stop without needing to taper down. Which is great news because it's bloody hard work, involves a lot of support and therefore costs a bomb.

Anyhow, I thought I could teach him the Tactical Change System while we were doing the detox.

Boy, was I wrong. Despite possessing a post-grad degree in a field of science I can't even pronounce, he just couldn't get the Tactical Change System into his head.

Why? Because managing your thoughts is nigh on impossible when you've been drinking. You simply don't have the self-awareness or the ability to make the mental effort.

You can't use the Tactical Change System to control alcohol. You can't control alcohol. It's like trying to control the falling of the leaves.

 You can never control alcohol: one is too many – a thousand is never enough.

But the decision is yours. I'm not going to tell you what to do, I'm not your dad. If I am, put down daddy's book and get back in bed this instant!

What I will tell you is this. If you think there's any chance that you'll ever stop drinking, then stop drinking *now*. If you think that you'll ever get to the point where some doctor will look you sternly in the eye and say, "Stop drinking", then stop drinking *now*.

It's like flying too close to the Death Star. When you first drift into its tractor beam you could fly off; you'd need to gun the engines, but you could do it. Yet there comes a point where you can't escape, where you're trapped in that tractor beam and, whether you like it or not, you're going to end up in the docking bay and possibly a trash compactor.

 There's a point of no return and you do not want to cross it.

My friend Jon knew he needed to stop drinking. He even stopped right at the end. But it was too late. He went past the point of no return.

You don't have to.

I wrote this book precisely to stop other men getting caught in the tractor beam. You're probably not there now, but if you keep drinking you will be. And then you'll end up dead even if you do stop drinking. That's what too late means.

Stop drinking. Now.

Feel the fear

Maybe you want to stop but you don't think you can. Obviously, it's not because you're scared. I mean, you're a roughty-toughty man's man. It's more that you don't feel ready. It's more that you're thinking, "Great, Duncan, all you've given me is Swiss army knife and I have to face the end of level boss".

Firstly, take a breath. Alcohol isn't an uber-baddy, it's an illusion. It's just Hank putting on his tough-guy voice.

And, secondly, the weapon doesn't matter. Removing the illusion of truth gives you a high-level skill set. Now your abilities are comparable to a Special Boat Service operator. Seeing the world as it really is; it's like learning to approach under cover of darkness, storm buildings and kick in doors.

Your tools are in your mind. Your tools are your strength and guile. You could blow up Hank with only household chemicals and a microwave.

You're in control now. That may surprise you, but only because your control has been slowly growing as you've been reading this book. You just didn't notice it.

You never notice gradual changes, that's why, if you gradually accelerate, you can end up driving well over the speed limit without your girlfriend freaking out. Remember your training and you will kick Hank's arse.

Nail your colours to the mast

The decision is yours. I won't make the decision for you. What I will do is urge you to make a decision. Pick a side, join a team, pin the badge over your heart and commit.

You need to commit, because this is what you're going to do for the rest of your life.

Either you spend the rest of your life living or you spend the rest of your life drinking. See it for what it is – the final, irreversible, life-long decision. Research has shown that people who make a decision that they believe they can't reverse are happier with their choice. So grab your courage and nail it to the sticking post.

And if you've decided that real men really do quit then this is what to do…

You already know

OK, you've probably guessed what I'm going to say, you've figured out the answer; you've worked out that pretty soon I'm going to tell you that every time that little voice says "you should have a drink," you're going to shout "Real Men Quit" in its face and do your best Zulu warrior victory dance.

It doesn't have to be that extreme. You could just think "Real Men Quit" and smile.

Simple. Best of all you know how it works. The Terminator, which is just Hank, says, "You should have a drink." That's the trigger.

THE DOOR MARKED EXIT

You think "Real Men Quit." That's the action. You smile. That's the celebration.

You reprogramme your brain. You never drink again. You're happy, strong, joyful, peaceful, free, powerful, energetic, focused and the sex is much better. The best bit is – I'm not lying about the last one.

WHY IT WORKS

B efore you take your final drink, let's make sure that you don't just know that it's going to work, you don't just feel that it's going to work, you know *why* it's going to work.

I know it works. I am standing before you today – well, sitting in a coffee shop months ago – as living proof that it works.

I never met him but I owe a huge debut to the world-renowned stop smoking expert Allen Carr – just for clarity, we aren't talking about the comedian. I don't think I can begin to put into words how much he changed my life. I couldn't have stopped smoking without his help and that's what started this crazy cascade of positive changes. I don't wish to over-apple the fruit salad but I'm pretty sure I owe him my life.

He knew it worked too. In fact, he proved it works on a global scale. Literally millions of people have stopped smoking by saying "Yippee, I'm a non-smoker". Although some of the youngsters might have baulked at yippee and changed it to "Sick, I'm a non-smoker cuz". As you can tell I have absolutely no idea how people talk these days and I'm going to sob a little because I feel so old.

For most people, the incredible worldwide success of Allen's method would be rock-solid proof that it actually works. Not academics of course. Academics want to pin it down, want to eliminate all of the random, unrelated factors. Because you've met so many people who've stopped smoking for random, unrelated factors.

Which is a tad over the top but you have to applaud their rigour. Anyhow, there's this guy called BJ Fogg who proved that everything Allen said was true. Best of all he did the proper psychologist stuff that makes peer-reviewed journal editors nod their heads sagely and agree that he is not speaking with forked tongue.

You already know the basis of BJ's work.

 Behaviour change is driven by triggers, actions and celebrations.

Partly you know that because I've been banging on about it for a hundred-odd pages and partly you know it because you've been living it your whole life.

More than just yippee

BJ puts a lot of stress onto the celebration part of the method. The good news is that you've been practising.

The bad news is that having worked with thousands of people around the world he learned which groups were best and worst at celebrating.

Terrible news: men aren't as good at celebrating as women. Even worse if, like me, you happen to be British. British men are almost the worst in the world at it. We managed to beat Japanese men, and I'm not sure that's much in the way of bragging rights.

Here's the headline.

 CELEBRATE!

Celebrate like your life depends on it, because sooner or later it might.

Celebrate good times, come on!

That sounds serious. Maybe you think you need an emergency celebration; you do, you need an SOS. Which stands for Save Our Celebrations. Look, it works if you say it out loud. It'll be awesome in the audio book. And you only need to remember the SAVE bit.

Because SAVE is a handy acronym to remember the four different areas that you could use to develop your own kick ass celebration routine.

S IS FOR STATE

Performance state imagery is a powerful technique, which is why many world-record smashing athletes swear by it. It's different from visualisation, which we'll come to, because it involves recapturing a previous achievement.

You celebrate by remembering a great moment from your past, such as a sporting win, nailing a presentation or kissing the prom queen. The trick is to recall it in as much detail as possible. In fact, to make the most of this technique it's worth practising. Find a quiet room and explore the incident in as much detail as possible – sights, smells, sounds and particularly emotions. Once you've practised it you can return to its warm embrace whenever you need to celebrate.

A IS FOR ACTION

If you're a hands-on guy, this one's for you. This can be any action that you'd use to celebrate: banging your chest like the silverback you are, or jumping up and down like no one is looking, or sliding into the corner flag on your knees. Please note that the latter is not appropriate for all surfaces.

There's some solid science behind this. A study with semi-pro football players showed that they performed better under pressure after having made a fist while practising. Raising your fist can make you better at penalties – are you listening, England footballers? It shows

that clenching your fist is powerful, activating the bits of your brain that you want pumping.

V IS FOR VISUALISATION

Which is just a fancy way of saying picturing a positive scene, this time imagined rather than real. From picturing yourself slamming the ball into the back of the net to clinch the World Cup final to receiving the Palm d'Or on your debut at Canne, it'll release the happy chemicals. If you want to picture a huge crowd chanting your name and throwing their underwear then knock yourself out.

It's easier than performance state imagery because you don't need to recall all the detail, just fantasise. But be careful if you're visualising that threesome with the oil-sleek Amazonians. Obvious and public erections don't lead to celebration, they lead to incarceration.

E IS FOR EXPRESSION

This is probably going to revolve around a smile. Just smile with your whole face, crease that forehead, raise those eyebrows, I want to see teeth damn it! Why not go for it? Why not giggle like a schoolgirl pumped full of nitrous oxide?

Happy or not, smiling releases dopamine and you know that dopamine is what makes learning work. Best of all, you can combine a smile with the other celebrations.

Use the Save Our Celebration system to craft the right celebration for you. The one that you'll enjoy, the one that'll stick. That way you can rewire your brain. And you don't even have to get the brown wire and the blue wire the right way around. You can do it by releasing the right chemicals at the right times.

Dopamine is your friend. Smile and learn, boys, smile and learn.

Who are you?

BJ Fogg uncovered another important part of the technique – identity. "I'm a non-smoker" sounds small and innocuous but there's huge power in that statement. It isn't "I'm not going to smoke" or "I don't smoke", or worst of all "I wish I didn't smoke". Those are all temporary states that could easily change. "I am a non-smoker" goes right down into the very core of who you are. Non-smokers don't smoke, ever. That's power.

When we get right down to the bottom of the well, who are you? Are you a drinker? Or are you someone who drinks but doesn't want to? How fundamental is drinking to who you are?

Let's look at it another way. Consider one of your other characteristics. You're generous, yes? You'd help out a mate in dire straits.

If I removed that sense of generosity you'd be diminished. You'd be less of a man. That's because being big-hearted is a part of who you are.

Is alcohol like that? If alcohol was removed from your life would you be diminished? Hell no, it's the opposite. You'd be a better version of yourself. You'd have more energy, focus and mental space to do the stuff that's a core part of your being.

What you're about to decide isn't simply drink or not drink, it's who you are. Are you going to embrace your better qualities or are you going to drown them in a waterfall of booze?

I cannot stress this enough.

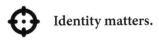 **Identity matters.**

Let's be clear then. You aren't *going to be* a real man. You don't *wish* you were a real man. It isn't one day, maybe, possibly, if it isn't too much trouble you're going to become a real man, perhaps. You *are* a real man, damn it! REAL. MAN. ROAR!!!

You're such a real man you probably jumped to your feet and let out a reverberating howl. Possibly you even ripped off your shirt. Maybe your girlfriend is now looking at you with a lustful glint in her eye. Good for you brother. You are a real man.

And real men quit.

" You gotta make way for the Homo Superior.

DAVID BOWIE

I swear the windows had got bigger. How else could you explain all the extra light that was radiating into the room? Come to think of it, there was more oxygen in the air. And a domestic phantom had done a bit of cleaning.

Things had changed.

Hank thumped down on the sofa, crossed his arms and harumphed. For all the world he looked like a teenager with a seriously parental problem.

I barely looked up from the book I'd lost myself in.

Hank uttered a diabolical oath under his breath.

I didn't respond.

He looked around the room, a desperation in his eyes. He scanned recklessly, hoping for something, anything.

"Pleeeease, can we go for a drink?" he asked.

I put the book down and met his gaze.

"You deserve a drink after all that reading," he said, "you'd better give your poor brain a rest, you're in serious danger of overheating your cognitive cantaloupe."

I just smiled. My eyes went to the page again.

"Oh, go on. We don't even have to go out, we could just grab a bottle. And maybe a hunk of cheese?"

Smile.

"I'm thirsty, muddy funster!"

I felt a bit sorry for him.

"Hank, I think you have a problem," I said.

"I don't have a problem, you have a problem."

"No, I had a problem, now I just have you." I said with a touch of vainglory.

"Son of a bitch, won't someone give me a goddam drink?"

"If only you could see the world as it truly is, Hank," I replied. "You see it through a glass darkly, but only because the glass is full of Guinness."

"Mmm Guinness," he closed his eyes wistfully.

Pity overtook me. Was I really like that? Just yesterday, barely 24 hours ago? Was I so enthralled by alcohol that I couldn't even smile without a drink?

"You know what I learned?" I asked.

We locked eyes and he shook his head with apprehension.

"Real. Men. Quit."

He groaned.

I leapt to my feet and started to dance. I was busting shapes, cutting the carpet and smouldering in the justified and ancient true groove. This was so not dad dancing.

"Get up, get on up, stay on the scene." I crooned like the godson of soul.

Hank did not move.

"Come on Hank, dance damn you."

He was still but I was shaking it like a polaroid picture.

"Celebrate, Hank. Laugh and dance and live and scream it with the whole of your soul..." I was spinning like a wild-ass flamenco conquistador. "Real! Men! Quit!" I wailed like a Hendrix guitar solo.

"I'm going to lie down," he said as he skulked out of the room.

I fell to the floor laughing and panting.

Real men quit. Real men dance. Real men live.

THAT LAST DRINK

Y ou understand alcohol. You understand the effect that it has on you, that it's been dragging you down for years. That it never got you over a single obstacle – in fact, it's your number one problem. You're thoroughly sick of it.

I have some great news. It's time to take your final drink.

As you're never going to drink again, this drink will mark the start of your new life. You're not going to think of it as the beginning of abstinence or the start of being deprived, because this is the start of your freedom from all the pain, regret, shame, sickness, embarrassment, stupidity and life-sucking misery that is alcohol.

Obligatory Medical Warning

You're a smart guy so you don't need this warning. But just in case this book happens to fall into the hands of any morons: in the unlikely event you experience a severe reaction to stopping drinking – such as chest pains, hallucinations or a seizure – don't be a dick, call a f*$king ambulance.

Goodbye

You should have your final drink in a specific way. Pour yourself a small shot of spirits – vodka, gin, rum, it doesn't matter but it has to be neat.

Find somewhere quiet where you can be on your own. Get yourself comfortable, leave your phone alone and relax.

Then take a sip of the spirit. Don't slam it, actually taste it and feel it. Taste how awful it is. Feel it roll down your throat like burning thunder. Allow yourself to experience how awful alcohol actually is, how awful it's always been.

Once you've taken that sip, slam down the glass and shout "Real Men Quit" at the top of your lungs. Pump your fist in the air like a provocatively-bearded revolutionary. Dance like the warrior gigolo that you are. Cheer like you've just been elected president of awesome, grand master of sublime and king of absolutely smashing the bejeezus out of life.

Or you could smile. Just make damn sure you celebrate.

 What you've done is worthy of celebration.

What's a celebration worth?

The best thing is the celebration doesn't have to stop there. You can keep it going.

Imagine that you checked your banking app and realised that someone had transferred £73,748.30 into your account. No mistakes, you get to keep it. How would you celebrate?

If you're thinking, "great, let's go down the pub and get trolleyed," it's time to think of a new way to celebrate. And you should celebrate because the thick end of £74 grand is only one bottle of wine or a four-pack of beer every day for the next twenty years. Someone has just put more than £73,748.30 in your bank account. Nice.

Which means you need to celebrate. You need to celebrate after saying "Real Men Quit", at a minimum a smile. You totally need to do that, but why not go further? Why not plan a proper celebration?

Celebration not inebriation

If you can only think of ways to celebrate that involve alcohol, then don't sweat it. Here's another way of approaching it.

ARE YOU REFLECTIVE?

You probably want to do something low-key. It could be taking a walk in the country or finding a nice view to stare at. It could be finding a quiet place, thinking about how great your life's going to be and saying "Real Men Quit" like a silent prayer. Let your inner peace beam out through a grin.

ARE YOU SOCIABLE?

Grab some friends – real friends, not drinking buddies. Arrange a meet up in a coffee shop or a restaurant, or even a bar if you're comfortable with that. Grab your coffee/OJ/mocktail/whatever and propose a toast. Which will obviously be shouting "Real Men Quit" and grinning like Mad Max with a tank full of petrol.

ARE YOU THE GUY THAT CAN'T SIT STILL?

Do something. It could be paintballing, bungee jumping or go-karting. I took my daughter to one of those trampoline parks the other day. I had more fun than she did. Or it could be purging your drinking-related stuff. Smashing things, pouring bottles down the sink, tearing out that Waikiki-themed bar you built in the shed. Once you're done, shout "Real Men Quit", grin like a madman and give it a good old jump around.

OR MAYBE YOU'RE DESPERATE?

Why not shell out three grand on an animatronic fornication doll with real effect breathing and a blowjob compatible head? Go

THAT LAST DRINK

165

wild, you get no judgement here [sniggering]. Or you could just buy a motorbike and find a real woman.

These celebrations are more involved. They require a bit of planning and maybe even some expense. And if you want a jelly-breasted sex-bot from China about four to six weeks delivery time – not that I looked. Don't skip it, you deserve it. You've worked hard; you're free. So celebrate.

One last time...

You don't need it but...

...I'm going to lay it on thick like tomato sauce: whatever happens to you, good times or bad times, whenever the idea of having a drink enters your mind, think "Real Men Quit" and smile.

 You got this.

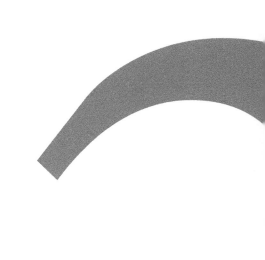

SECTION

Choose New Actions

" When they kick at your front door, how you gonna come?

Paul Simonon

God I hate this sort of thing.

I had managed to walk through the door. I only did it because the desire to start my own business outweighed my fear of talking to people I haven't met. Part of me knew that surprisingly few networking events end in humiliation, expulsion from the tribe and the slow and lonely ordeal that is death by starvation.

What was the worst that could happen? I could stand in the corner on my own, drinking tea and failing to make friends in a room full of people trying to sell stuff. Not technically that bad.

"Alwight," said a contradiction. He sounded like a dole scrounging chav yet he was dressed like a country gent. I'm not, as a rule, judgy but I wasn't sure I liked either alternative.

"Hi," I replied with a hint of doubt.

"People call me Smiffy," he smiled. "Mostly 'cause it annoys me."

"People call me Duncan, mostly because I don't respond to Gobby McGob-Shite".

He smiled. I was starting to think that today might not be so bad.

And it wasn't. After working our way through our CVs, the Clash's back catalogue and several cups of tea I discovered that he used to be a drinker.

"Really?" I asked.

"Oh yeah, I used to be a proper scrote, drinkin' cider out of a big plastic bottle and smokin' dog ends off the floor, I even had a goldie lookin' chain."

"That seems hard to believe. You're so successful."

"Yeah, well, I've travelled a long way but trust me, there was a time when I would have sold your grandmother for a drink."

"My grandmother?"

"Yeah, it'd have to be yours, I already sold mine."

I thought that was nearly as funny as he did.

"What did you do? I mean, to change so much, what's the secret?"

"It's not a secret. Keep movin'."

"All you did was put one foot in front of the other? Solve one problem after another?"

"Abso-bloody-lutely. Drinkin' was a problem, I solved it. Smokin' was a problem, I solved it. Dress sense was a problem..." He looked down at his tweed get up. "And I'm workin' on it!"

I couldn't help but grin.

"You took your biggest problem and solved it. Once you'd solved that you discovered a new problem, so you solved that?"

"Pretty much. But do you want to know the best thing?"

"I imagine I do."

"Now my problems are sweeeeeet." he said with a beam. "Now my biggest problem is do I put the money in my pension or do I take it out of the business and waste it on a vintage pinball machine?"

"Nice problem to have."

"Man, that's all success is. Better problems."

I thought about that. Maybe I didn't want to live without problems, maybe problems where my friend. Maybe stress was a good sign.

I needed to up my game, elevate my thinking and start smashing the shit out of life.

What I needed was some better problems...

REAL MEN FEEL THE FORCE

You may legitimately be wondering what you're still doing here. You've stopped drinking, job done. You're wondering why you have to read more words? Simple. Stopping is easy. It's staying stopped that's the trick.

 Real men don't just quit. Real men stay quit.

Which I'm guessing you're on board with. You didn't want an Elastoplast for a broken leg. You didn't want a makeshift bodge job. You want something that will last like the reign of Elizabeth II. If you wanted a flash in the pan, you'd have bought *Real Men Dabble*. So, you're keen to get on and do some more reading.

And if you're not, I'll let you in on a little secret. This is where the magic happens. This is where you step into your power and bestride the river of true manhood.

We're, therefore, going to bump up against the question of what makes a man real. And I'm going to answer it with that age-old bit of wisdom that all the sages inevitably run to: it depends. But we'll get into that. For the moment let's look at one aspect of being a real man we can all agree on. Without a doubt, Jedi equals real man.

Real Jedi Quit

Jedi is a concept you understand. But it isn't a concept George Lucas invented. Jedi are simply warrior poets, and they're as old as humanity itself. They bring balance. They're light and dark, yin and yang, strength and understanding, creation and destruction. It's the *balance* that's the key.

Think about it, what's the difference between Luke Skywalker and Darth Vader? Just in case it's been a while since you watched the films, Luke's the goody and Darth's the baddy – but it goes so much deeper than that.

The difference is the characteristics they embody. Darth Vader is all about strength and order. Luke has strength and order too but for Darth, that's all he's got. Darth is limited to strength and order: Luke has more.

Luke has feeling and understanding. That's what Old Ben and Yoda are trying to drill into his head – *feel* the force. It's about feeling, not about acting or powering through. It's about seeing the world for what it is, rather than trying to bend it to your will. You can't grab the force in the same way you can't put love in a box. And no, a fleshlight doesn't count as love in a box.

Luke wins not because he's stronger but because he has greater feeling and understanding. That's the force.

And that's what you must embrace.

Cool, right? Not just stopping drinking but Jedi training too.

Bring the balance

You might have heard of Carl Jung, if you haven't, he's a bit like Sigmund Freud but without the penis obsession. He's basically one of those dudes that did psychology way before business gurus started banging on about it.

He wrote a lot, much of which is impenetrable, but to put it simply he thought that strength and order are generally masculine traits and that feeling and understanding are often feminine traits. I'm not suggesting you categorise people according to the views of some dead

pipe-smoking savant, but you recognise the strong, ordered man and the woman who feels and understands.

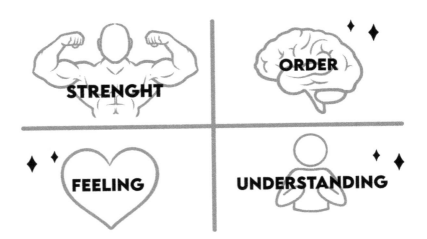

The trick is to go beyond your starting point. Rather than looking for feeling and understanding in women, men should look for it in themselves. To become a complete human being, you need to embrace what you lack.

That's the real difference between Luke and Darth. Darth thinks strength and order is enough, but Luke realises that it's all about harmony. To bring balance to the universe you must first bring balance to yourself. That means you must get what you don't have.

That's what being a Jedi Knight is about: it's knowing you have the strength to destroy but the feeling to appreciate what that destruction will mean, and the understanding to see when it's right to use your strength. Creation. Destruction. Balance.

The lost equilibrium

Alcohol upsets the balance. It's like a gradually-increasing weight that grows and grows until it dominates your life. For me, it started off as something occasional, something for the odd weekend. But by the end it pressed onto everything, it had come to overburden every decision, every waking movement. On one side was the gargantuan presence of booze, on the other everything else was squeezed in. The balance was gone.

Worse than that, it unbalanced my personality. It gave me a false belief in strength. It made me feel superhuman. It made me feel like I could take on the world. That feeling came after the first bottle and it disappeared the next morning but, for an hour or so, I felt like the most powerful person on the planet. But I was weak.

I was convinced I had everything in order. That's because I got great at ignoring the mayhem. I'd simply move on. It was as if I'd written "order" on a scrappy piece of paper and pinned it on to the disorder.

It also inhibited my ability to understand the world around me. It prevented me from understanding the people I loved. Because part of my mind was always wondering where the next drink was coming from, I couldn't really listen, I couldn't really understand what people needed. Think about it for a second: alcohol stops your brain from working properly. What does that do to your understanding?

Alcohol's effect on feelings was the biggie. Alcohol fundamentally affects them. Some people believe it blunts your emotions – in fact, some people think that's the main benefit of drinking. But it doesn't blunt your emotions. It sloshes them around. They don't disappear, they trickle off into another pond as you drink the first bottle. Once you're halfway through the second they come flooding back.

Alcohol doesn't stop you feeling, it delays it. And during that delay the pressure builds. Once the gates open, the deluge comes.

All the areas of your life that matter are hampered by alcohol. All the things you need to work on to bring balance to your life are hampered by alcohol. Everything you did during your drinking life was hampered by alcohol.

 You can't do anything about the past.
But you can control the future.

Warfare? Poetry?

You need to bring the balance you need to embrace your inner Jedi. Use your newfound energy and focus to add. Take your undeniable strength and add order, add understanding, add feeling. Use the force. That's what real men do.

And take a moment to celebrate. It's amazing that you've got here. You're starting to really change your life. The booze was dragging you down but now you're going to start to fly.

But maybe there's doubt. Maybe you think men don't do poetry? Men don't understand. Men definitely don't cry and feel and care. That's women stuff. Me want meat.

But that's an illusion. Actually it's probably an excuse, the kind of weak excuse that men use to justify sneaking off to the pub and leaving the women to do all the real work.

I'm not going to trot out all of my views about how biology is flexibility and how two million years of hominid existence proves that. My views aren't important. It's what you think that counts. You've come so far breaking down alcohol's illusion of truth. Maybe that's helped you to see other glaring illusions, and there are many in our society.

I don't want you to sleepwalk through life. I want you to wake up, smell the coffee, shout "Real Men Quit" and start to see the world as it really is. And that involves waking up to the fact that seeing male and female as opposites is a big, fat illusion of truth.

Don't relive school discos

Masculinity and femininity aren't opposites. They aren't even a spectrum. It's more like a splatter-painting of traits. Some men like guns, some women like makeup. But there are men who like makeup and women who like guns. Liking guns doesn't make women less feminine. I mean, Princess Leia is firing a blaster on the original poster for *A New Hope*. Do you think less of her? No, you think she's smoking hot! And if you happen to like makeup then there will be plenty of women queuing up, because women really dig that sort of thing. Well, some of them.

This is backed up by a meta-analysis, a study of studies, published in *The American Psychologist*. It looked at 46 studies that measured things like: maths and science ability, vocabulary and talkativeness, spatial awareness, negotiation and aggression, leadership skills, helping behaviour, morality and cheating, body image and even smiling. In short, a bunch of stuff that you'd happily chuck into male and female piles.

Yet what it found was very little difference between men and women. About the only areas that men stood out in were ball-throwing and masturbation. I'm guessing you agree with both of those conclusions.

It also found that if you took a random man and a random woman and ran the tests, about 40% of the time the man's score would be more "feminine" than the woman's.

If you conform to the masculine stereotype you're the exception not the rule. If you're only into boobs, cars and football then you're the freak. Join the normal people – take up crochet.

It's OK, you don't have to crochet, and you don't have to stop liking boobs (hooray for boobies). What you need to do is beat down the illusion of truth that men are on one side and women are on the other and there's zero crossover. That hasn't been true since you stopped going to school discos.

Embrace what you lack, even if that's feelings. It's the path to becoming a Jedi. *Feel* the force.

YOU'RE NUMBER ONE

There's a reason why the sprawling *Star Wars* universe couldn't just be contained in one film. True, at the end of *A New Hope* Luke was looking pretty Jedi but he wasn't done. He went on to learn more, in the swamps with Yoda and on the Death Star. Yet he still wasn't done.

He kept learning as he instructed Rey – heck, he kept developing after he died. That's the power of the force.

While I'm not exactly promising you immortality, I can promise you that becoming a Jedi isn't a one-and-done thing. It isn't like you can say "I got my lightsabre, that's me, I am Jedi". Do you think my buddy who spent £200 on a toy lightsabre has suddenly become a real Jedi? Real idiot possibly. No, he has a lot of work still to do.

Stopping drinking is the same. It's no good thinking "I've stopped, great, I'm going to go back to doing everything I did before," because you'll end up drinking again.

Stopping is a step in a recipe, it's not the whole meal. Being awesome is not a blue moon, almost never, odd job. It's more like dental hygiene.

 Successes are like teeth. If you don't keep brushing you lose them.

Stopping is easy. It's staying stopped that's the trick. Real men don't just quit. Real men don't just stay quit. Real men bring balance to themselves. Real men become Jedi. The balance surrounds you and penetrates you: deep inside you know this.

Theoretical to practical

If you consider where I was when I was drinking, it wouldn't take too much imagination to see that alcohol was my number one problem. I solved it. Which meant that I had one less problem, but I hadn't really done much. A new number one problem stepped up and started to dominate the landscape. Hank said, "Thank you very much" and I started to eat a bunch of junk food.

Once I solved the problem of alcohol my life became dominated by the problem of pre-packaged pretend meals. Without being aware of it I'd slipped easily into a different number one problem. That's not uncommon. Far too many people swap booze for food, or work, or Facebook or the gym. It means that you can boil life right down to five words:

 Solve your number one problem.

And the thing about number one problems is that they keep coming. I stopped drinking and my new number one problem was my diet. I stopped eating pre-chewed food and my new number one problem was finding a way not to starve. I started to eat a whole food, plant-based diet and my new number one problem was the idiot boss at my imbecilic job. I moved on to...

You get the idea. I kept moving. I kept solving my number one problem.

Filling up the nothingness

Some people worry that stopping drinking will leave a gaping hole in their life, that something will be missing. They may then interpret

the need to solve problems as the need to do something to fill up the empty space vacated by booze.

Really? Do you think you're going to miss all those fun times? Like when you drank piss out of a rugby boot. Great times. I can really see how you'd miss that.

Of course you know that booze never filled a hole. You know that drinking never did anything for you. You know that it never provided you with pleasure, it only ever held you back. It stopped you becoming the man you need to be.

Getting rid of it can't have left a hole. Deep inside you already realise that stopping drinking doesn't create a pit of Sarlacc, alcohol *is* the pit of Sarlacc.

You're not keeping busy in some desperate attempt to fill up a yearning void. You're moving forward to escape from the ravenous, multi-tentacled, sand-pit beast that is booze.

You may have more time but only because you used to waste so much of it drinking. Don't see it as a hole – it's not a depression. It's the opposite, it's an explosion of great stuff. It's possibly the greatest opportunity you'll ever get.

Why not go on an amazing journey? You might as well jump on your bike and pedal through the most inspiring countryside, with fascinating people, stopping to sample delectable food and after lunch go for a skinny-dip in a dazzling pool in a mystical, sunlit bower.

You might as well because that, my friends, that's your life.

Solve your number one problem

Now I want to make it very clear that I didn't solve all of my problems in a couple of days. I kept solving my number one problem slowly, over the course of a few years. I made mistakes. I didn't always get it right, I understand now that a business selling crumpets as hotdog buns was a stupid idea, even if Crump-dogs™ sounded cool.

During the difficult times, the times when people ridiculed my griddle-bread business model, I always returned to a quote from Luke Skywalker: "Get back up. Always get back up." You can't solve your biggest problem if you've fallen on your arse.

REAL MEN QUIT

And you can't solve them all at once.

Please consider all of the advice contained in the next few chapters as *advice*. It's not meant to be done all at once, or even that quickly. Heck, some of it you won't even need to do at all.

And if you screw up any of it, just remember Crump-dogs™ and "Get back up. Always get back up."

It's absolutely essential that you don't think "I can't meditate, write a gratitude journal and make smoothies so I'm going to give up and drink myself stupid".

If your number one problem happens to be focus, consider mediation. If it's overthinking consider journaling. If it's nutrition buy a blender. If it's all of those, just remember, you don't have to do everything today. You just have to keep at it. (Full disclosure, I do not meditate, write a gratitude journal or drink smoothies. I solve number one problems.)

When should I start?

When's the best time to act? Now! Heck, the only time to act is now. Look at the clock – the big hand is pointing to now and the little hand is pointing to now.

Get started. What you can do this very second is stop saying, "Real Men Quit" when you have your morning coffee. You don't need it anymore. Sure, you need to say it when your brain suggests you drink some alcohol. In fact, you must.

But saying it with your coffee has served its purpose. Why not use that time for something better?

Tomorrow morning, instead of saying "Real Men Quit" and doing an insane punk pogo dance, try saying "You're number one!". True, you'll doubtless say, "Real Men Quit, I mean You're number one!", but that's OK.

I feel I ought to point out what a great phrase "You're number one!" is. It reminds you to solve your number one problem but it also reminds you that you *are* number one. And you are, you're rockin' the main stage in the Mos Eisley Cantina, whoop whoop, siren emoji and everything.

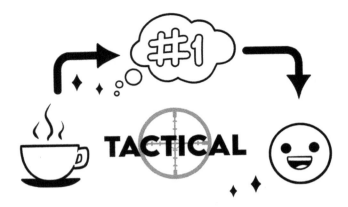

Your New Hope

Becoming a Jedi involves more than moving away from your old life: it's about going towards a new one. And the key word in that sentence is *new*.

When someone has stopped drinking, the world is apt to say that they've recovered. But recovery implies that you're going back to where you were before you had that first drink. Do you want to go back to where you were?

When I started drinking, I was spotty, I knew nothing about the world yet I thought I was a genius. I had a patchy relationship with the shower and no relationship with the opposite sex. Was that where I wanted to go back to? Do you think I yearn for the excitement of wanking over the frilly knickers in the Kays catalogue? Hell no!

I wanted to develop. I wanted to be something new. I wanted to be a Jedi. The last thing I wanted to do was to recover what I had. I wanted revolution.

 We don't do recovery. We do progress.

We don't do returning to where we once were. We do finding something new. And to do that we solve number one problems. You're number one.

> ## " I'll tell you this, no eternal reward will forgive us now for wasting the dawn.

JIM MORRISON

The cars were sluggish, the rain was busy. I'd been on this road for hours and I'd probably be here for hours more. I was unmoved. I was beyond late but it wasn't tugging at my tattered soul.

I knew that until recently it would have. A few weeks ago, I would have been livid. I would have stewed like a pot full of barley and vegetables. But not today.

Today I was happy just to be. And that sense of being took my gaze to the passenger seat, which took me all the way to a Scottish road I'd travelled down back in the times before...

Jon and I rented a cottage on the outskirts of nowhere. It wasn't just a long drive, it was a long drive after we'd crossed the Scottish border.

We left early so Jon had been precisely no help. The second we got into the car he'd fallen asleep and stayed that way. He'd woken up in a service station somewhere around Perth. And he was hungry.

Rather than getting a Big Mac, like any normal human traveller, he'd opted for a self-heating meal. Which came in a can. As we set off he'd started the heating process.

"Duncan," he said in a worried tone.

"What?" I replied.

"It's getting hot."

"It's a self-heating meal."

"Yeah but it's getting too hot to hold."

"Put it down then."

He looked around the car. There was no obvious space to put a hunk of metal that was undergoing an internal chemical reaction resulting in an ever-rising temperature.

"It's getting really hot," he said with some desperation.

I laughed.

I probably shouldn't have but his scruffy, panicking face was kind of amusing in its desperation.

He laughed too. It's amazing what a sizable dose of the ridiculous can do for rapidly burning fingers.

We laughed. Too much.

I could barely see through the tears. Which isn't the best way to hammer down a twisting mountain road at a shade over sixty.

I laughed again.

I laughed as I remembered his big unkempt face. I laughed as I remembered the stupidity of it all. I laughed at the weird, complex, muddled up, beauty of his life.

I looked out at the multiverse of cars blocking my route home. The journey would have been more fun if Jon was here. It wasn't so much that he'd have done something entertaining, more that something entertaining would have been done to him by a universe that was clearly out to lunch.

If I'd had the chance I would have chosen a different path for him. But it was never my choice. Maybe there was something else I could have done but I doubt it would have made much difference.

Jon's life was his life, I couldn't change that. All I could do was remember how much I enjoyed it. How lucky I was to be a part of it. How, given a thousand lifetimes, I would choose to be his friend again and again and again, despite the loss, despite the pain.

What were a few cars between me and home? What were a few hours of delay? What were the minor inconveniences of life compared to the beauty and splendour that we had shared together.

I may as well just sit back and enjoy it. I wasn't on a motorway, I was on a spring-warm Scottish hillside, heather flower fragrance drifting into my olfactory receptors.

I may as well just lie here, a sprawling meadow, beneath the trees, a lonely cloud in the breeze.

REAL MEN ARE STRONG

Let me lay it on as thick as I can: what I'm about to outline is a whole heap of work. A life's work, for want of a better phrase. You don't have to do it all this week or this year. Actually, you don't ever have to do all of it.

You have to solve your number one problem. Once you've solved that, you'll have a new number one problem. Solve that. Repeat.

We're going to start with strength. The basis of your strength is your body, we're going to get physical.

There are a number of annoying little issues that can come out of stopping drinking. These might include stomach problems, appetite issues, a desire for sugary food, rashes, sweating, constipation or generally feeling a bit unusual. If you experience any of these, and they're by no means universal, don't panic, they're normal. You should go to the doctor. As you're a man you won't. So, if it doesn't get better in a week…

Go. To. The. Doctor.

If nothing else, you'll get to smugly tell them that you've stopped drinking!

Power up

Your body is amazing. I'm not hitting on you, that's just a biological fact. The way everything inside it interacts is enormously complex; what it does is akin to doing keepie-uppies while solving a cryptic crossword.

Just think about how diet, exercise and sleep combine. Eating a poor diet will destroy your motivation to exercise and disturb your sleep. Getting a bad night's sleep will mean you have no energy to exercise and you'll make bad food choices. And if you don't exercise you won't be tired, and you'll feel bad about eating a large meat feast pizza. It's connected like a slick-backed mafioso.

The way these things work together is mind-bendingly complicated. Which might make you want to throw up your hands and grab a beer. But I suggest you smile because the interaction is good. If you do one good thing, it leads to another. Get better sleep and you get more energy, but it also balances your blood sugars which means you make better food choices. The way it builds up is complex but who cares? It builds and that's why if you start going in the right direction you'll tend to continue in the right direction.

Quick win

You're probably mildly dehydrated. A recent survey showed that just 6% of British people are hydrating properly. Mind you, the survey was done by a mineral water company. It might not be pure science.

That said, you probably don't drink enough. You should drink 250ml per 10 kilos of body weight. If you weigh anything approaching 80 kg (or 12 ½ stone) you should be drinking about two litres a day. If you're drinking less, then drink more.

And it's easy. It's a ridiculously quick win. After all, the one skill you've developed over the years is pouring stuff down your throat. Sadly, coffee doesn't count, even if you shout "hydrate!" while you do it.

Virtuous sleep cycle

When I stopped drinking, I was petrified that I wouldn't be able to sleep. I mean, for years I hadn't fallen asleep normally. Every night I was blacking out rather than drifting off. So I was worried if I'd be able to sleep. Add to that the fact that I was under the impression that I suffered from insomnia.

What I now realise is that it wasn't insomnia, it was smoking. Nicotine is a powerful stimulant; smoking before bed messes with your sleep. I know that now but at the time I just thought I was an insomniac. I worried.

Luckily, I didn't worry that much, I didn't turn it into a thing. The day I stopped drinking I thought it might take a while to nod off, so I grabbed a book on the way to bed. I settled in and started reading. I was asleep in minutes.

I'm not saying you have to read sci-fi before bed, but I am saying you should seriously consider a routine.

Now, that might all sound a touch juvenile; "come on Johnny it's your bedtime". You're a grown-up, I get that – you can stay up late if you want to. But going to bed at the same time, at least on school nights, has been proven to be beneficial. Research done by Duke Medical School found that irregular sleep patterns were linked with heart disease, obesity, diabetes and being a dull boy.

Adding a pre-bed routine to a regular bedtime has also been shown to reduce stress. And you don't need me to tell you that stress equals bad sleep. Even if you can't explain the exact pathway of the neurotransmitters, you've done your fair share of lying in bed at night stressing about what your idiot boss did. Even a short routine will put some space between bed and the stress of the day.

Best of all you're already doing it. You already check the alarm, clean your teeth, go to the loo and put on your Ewok pyjamas, and you do it in an order – you already have a routine. Expand it a bit. Add some light stretching, some caffeine-free tea, a bath, maybe a spot of gratitude. Most of all try to do it at the same time every evening, or at least five of seven evenings a week.

And don't forget a good book. Reading makes people feel tired, if you're planning to try it, I can recommend some proper awesome sci-fi. Seriously, get in touch – I'm reading something amazing at the moment that I'd love to share. Just put Bhaskaran Brown into google and you'll find me.

The symphony of nutrition

Clearly, sleeping wasn't my number one problem. Luckily, my number one problem was already pretty obvious.

Thanks to my commitment to rock n roll excess, I'd given myself gout. This is an impressive achievement for an average boy from a town in what was once Berkshire. Gout used to be the disease of kings. I felt it was a clear demonstration that I was living the high-life – heck, gout is so jet-set.

The problem is that it hurts. It hurt so much that I went to the doctor. Obviously, the doctor said I needed to take medication for the rest of my life. That's what doctors do: give it a Latin sounding name and prescribe a pill.

When I stopped drinking it definitely got better. This isn't surprising because a review of all the science published in 2011 found that alcohol increased the risk of gout. But I wasn't happy with improvement. I wanted cure. Clearly, my doctor didn't see that on the cards but that didn't worry me because he went to medical school when bloodletting was a cutting-edge therapeutic approach.

I did my research and found that many studies showed a link between meat and gout. This made me think about my diet, which was a bit Homer Simpson. During my drinking days I considered kebabs to be a late-night light bite. And since I'd stopped I'd decided that, as I no longer drank, I could eat whatever I wanted.

This might not have been the best decision. While I felt amazing since I'd stopped poisoning myself with alcohol, my diet was definitely holding me back. The gout was just a part of the problem; there were also issues with energy, sex-drive and obviously weight. Gout was just the most obvious one because it hurt. I'm not joking, it's really painful. I came to the conclusion that it was time to change my diet. I'd walked slap bang into my number one problem.

I took everything I'd learnt about drinking, everything I'd learnt about Hank, automatic thinking, cognitive dissonance, about the illusion of truth and I applied it to food. In short, I used Belief Disposal and Tactical Change to transform my diet.

It worked. I stopped having gout. And I lost a ton of weight. And I started to wear the same size of trousers I wore in my twenties. And I felt all springy and lithe like I was a shorter version of Legolas without the ears. I felt amazing.

I'd solved my number one problem.

Cue the next problem

Diet sorted, tick. Gout cured, tick. Problem solved, tick. Yet...

I had a new number one problem. Physically my problem was now exercise, or the lack of it. Now, I don't want you to think that I stopped drinking, stopped eating junk, cured my gout and looked at my life and thought "everything is perfect, I need a spot of jogging". My biggest issue was actually something else but we're talking about strength so let's pretend for a second.

We all know we should exercise. Some people appear to enjoy it, others not so much. If you're in the first camp it won't be a problem. If you're like me then it may take a bit of strength to turn that nagging doubt that you should exercise into actual sweat.

I started by thinking about the best time to do it. I concluded that it was first thing in the morning. I decided to do it before I was really awake, before I had a chance to change my mind. I also thought about the smallest amount of exercise that I get away with. I chose High Intensity Interval Training (HIIT) because you can achieve something in five minutes if you go for it. Then I went for it. And then I celebrated.

Tactical workout

I've managed to maintain it. Yes, I even did it this morning. Because I have a good system.

I picked a regular trigger – after all, I get up every day. I picked an achievable action – five minutes of HIIT. And then I celebrated. I do a stupid dance at the end of my workout, but you could smile. Then again, maybe I'm starting to have an effect on you; maybe the desire to dance is growing. Maybe you're starting to become a little bit Duncan – maybe this time next week you'll be as annoyingly positive as me?

Either way the celebration primed my brain to start the tracking. Trigger. Action. Celebration. Tracking. Tick, tock, tactical.

Start small, pick a trigger, go for it, be happy.

 Your brain will do the rest.

Chips with everything

Maybe you don't like the sound of HIIT. Maybe you wonder what makes a good action. In short, chips. I don't mean you should always eat chips when you get out of bed – that way disaster lies. What I mean is you should serve CHIPS with everything. Obviously CHIPS is a handy acronym.

In deference to our American friends, I should point out that I mean French Fries, not chips. What they call chips, I call crisps. Look, to avoid confusion I mean potatoes cut into chunks and deep fried. Sod it, let's get to it.

C FOR CLEAR

Your action needs to be precise and solid. The action isn't exercise, that's too vague. The action is 5 minutes of HIIT. Make your actions clear; this will help them become automatic. If you have to figure out what to do every time it'll never automate.

H FOR HONEST

There is no point in me aiming to do an hour of free weights. That isn't honest. I can manage about 4 minutes of that before I give up and start playing solitaire on my phone. Be honest. The best action is the one you actually do.

I FOR IF/THEN

You remember this from earlier. You can create Terminator-style automation in your head by using If/Then coding. The trigger is the If and the action is the Then. That's the only way the system works. If: getting out of bed, Then: exercise. If: writing a book, Then: add weak jokes. If/Then coding automates.

P FOR POSITIVE

Is exercise positive? Yes, in the sense of a good thing to do, not in the sense of hurrah, sweat and pain. All of your actions should be positive in that way. Even if you want to stop doing something it should be positive. The phrase is not "don't drink", it's "Real Men Quit". If the action isn't positive, it makes the celebration hard. Always frame your actions in a positive way – "You're number one!".

S FOR SELF

It has to be something that you would do. It has to be not just honest but a part of who you are. We don't say "isn't it great I don't have to drink", we say "Real Men Quit", because we're real men. That's not just how we roll, it's who we are. Obviously don't get hung up on trying to work out which kind of exercise defines you as a person. Just consider if you're more bench pressing or body popping.

When you start to design your own habits don't forget to shove some CHIPS on the side of the plate. That'll turn it into a meal rather than a snack. That'll sate your hunger for change.

The second worst drug you take

Do you smoke? If so, I have some advice for you.

Don't.

Do you vape? If so, I have some advice for you. You know what's coming, right? Don't do it man!

As I have yet to write *Real Men Quit (Cigarettes)*, here's what I suggest. Spend a moment thinking about everything you've read. Do you think everything I've said about drinking applies to smoking or vaping? Think about the illusion of truth: about how alcohol helps you handle stress, about how alcohol helps you to socialise, about how alcohol makes you a real man. Do you think those apply to smoking and vaping?

Isn't it the case that smoking and vaping cause you stress? Isn't it the case that because you have to go outside it spoils social occasions? Isn't it the case that because smoking and vaping makes you a slave to nicotine it's getting in the way of your being a man?

You've broken the illusion of truth about alcohol. Now break the illusion of truth about smoking and vaping. Challenge your assumptions.

REAL MEN ARE STRONG

193

Then change your thinking. Use the Tactical Change System to disrupt your thoughts about smoking or vaping. Every time you think about it, that's the trigger. The action is to shout, "Real Men Quit (cigarettes)." The celebration can be whatever you want, use the Save Our Celebrations System.

Whatever form it takes, the celebration creates the happy brain chemicals and that creates the tracking. Then you start to notice the triggers even more and you've created an attention loop. Trigger, Action, Celebration, Tracking. Boom! Tactical.

Once you've done that, choose new actions. Which is what you're doing, Trust me, smoking or vaping is your number one problem. Solve. Smile. You're number one.

And overwhelm

We've covered strength, we've looked at hydration, sleep, diet, exercise, smoking, vaping, and now you're completely overwhelmed. Your to-do list contains slightly less pages than *Lord of the Rings* but feels like hiking to Mount Doom while being chased by the fighting Uruk-Hai.

Breathe.

If you've had about a million ideas about what you could do, make it real simple. Put the book down. Think about what you've read. Are any of these problems your number one problem? If yes – solve now. If no – solve when it becomes your number one problem.

 If you keep going even the annoying little things become number one problems.

Incidentally, did you say "You're number one!" when you had coffee this morning? No? Is that because you're enjoying the book so much you've been reading all night and haven't gone to bed? Or because you bellowed "Real Men Quit" and jumped on the table?

Either way, don't sweat it. Try again tomorrow.

And remember, Belief Disposal and Tactical Change have power. Are you beginning to see just how much?

REAL MEN HAVE ORDER

 rder is a little less obvious. What does it mean? CEOs have order. Companies don't lose money because of a lack of strength, it's a lack of order. Order makes money. But soldiers have order too. You don't forget your helmet because you lack strength, it's a lack of order. Order saves lives.

There are two levels of order. There's the outward expression of order, the bits people can see. Is your house tidy? Are you good at your job? Have you forgotten your trousers again? Then there's the internal order that you can't see.

> **The ordered mind is the sign of the true Karma Kommando.**

Let's start with the external stuff, but don't worry – what follows isn't a treatise on cleaning your house. If you want that then Marie Kondo is your woman; she's odd, mystical and strangely hot all at the same time.

What we're going to look at is the truly important stuff. Your fortune, your family and your friends.

Real men quit (their job)

After I'd stopped drinking, reformed my diet and cured my gout, I looked at the rest of my life. Like many ex-drinkers I discovered wreckage. Don't get me wrong, I was a high-functioner, I had the alcoholic platinum card and everything. But it only seemed like it all worked because I talked a good game. Below the facade was subsidence.

There were many things that needed tidying up but the most pressing was undoubtedly my work life. I'd been at war with my boss for the last year.

He was a borderline sociopath who only cared about his own success, the kind of fiend who outsourced his kids to some scary lady he found on Fiverr. Needless to say, I'd stopped enjoying my job years ago.

Why had I continued to work there for all that time? Simple. I could do it with a hangover. Once I stopped feeling rough every morning, I started to feel that there may be more to life than this. I decided to fire my boss.

I'd discovered my new number one problem.

I started to look for a new job. Part of me was desperate to sabotage that; I clung to the few small advantages that my job offered. It was close to home, it was easy, I could live on the money, it was two doors down from Greggs.

And how many people have you met like that? The ones that cling to a job they hate because they're too scared to venture out of their comfort rut. It's a lot like the fear of a sober life – as long as you buy into the illusion that you can't find anything better you'll remain weak. You're worth more.

True, I was scared but I found some things to apply for and, more by luck than judgement, I managed to get hired. Goodbye to the job I hated. Goodbye to the idiot boss.

I had to work less time for more money and my boss wasn't a cretinous clodpoll. True, he wasn't exactly Obi Wan, but it was a step in the right direction. I moved on and I didn't look back. Because if you look back while you're walking away there's a good chance you'll trip over.

People not positions

There was of course a deeper level of order that needed to be addressed. Relationships.

Throughout my drinking career I'd been selfish. I put booze ahead of my wife. I prioritised doing things that allowed me to drink over what she needed. I'd invested more in my relationship with Hank than the one with her.

Man, am I lucky that she's a very enlightened human being. She stuck by me. In fact, it was her gently nudging me that started all this quitting malarkey in the first place.

It dawned on me that if I didn't do something there would be no one to celebrate the joy of going beyond booze with. I needed to do something to hold on to our relationship because if I didn't, there would be no one to listen to me going on about how much better my new boss was. I mean, Steve was a great guy – he had a black belt in Taekwondo and everything.

I'd go as far as to say that it started to feel like a number one problem. I invested some of my new-found time and energy into our relationship. We did things together, although probably not as much as we should have. We talked, although probably not as much as we should have. I even cleaned the flat, definitely not as much as I should have – Marie Kondo I ain't. But it was a start.

As our relationship began to flourish again, she got pregnant. After months of vacillating between fear and excitement our daughter Leela was born. And that brought a whole new set of number one problems. But that's a different book, possibly called *Real Men Quit Only Being a Father When It Fits Around Their Job, the Football and Sitting Down for a Bit.*

Mates make the world go around

What about friends? The men I help often ask if they should spend time with people who drink. That's an easy question to answer. If you enjoy spending time with them, then spend time with them. If you don't, stop returning their calls.

I'm a morris dancer. I'm not embarrassed by that, it just hasn't come up in conversation yet. If you aren't snickering then let me explain. Morris dancing is a form of folk dance that involves hankies. It also involves heavy drinking – that's why I started. When I stopped drinking I carried on dancing because it turns out that I enjoy it and I like the blokes I dance with. Amazingly, it was never about the drink.

That said, there were some people I only used to drink with; we had nothing else in common. I don't spend time with them anymore.

In short, I have zero desire to drink, so I don't mind spending time with people who are drinking – actually, I love it because I get to shout "Real Men Quit" in my head and smile a lot. But I only do it with people I like.

Now you have the choice. You don't have to go to the pub to hang out with people who drink more than you simply to feel good about yourself. But you can if they're fun to be with.

Maybe you're a little worried about going to the pub because of the allure of all that booze. Think of it like this, if you went to a strip club you'd be tempted by the naked women because you desire them. For old you the pub was like a giant titty-bar. But new you doesn't desire booze so it's like going to the zoo. You don't get a hard on looking at a giraffe.

Without desire, there is no temptation.

Only rude to the people we like

There's probably also a little concern about how your friends are going to treat you. And by a little concern I mean a tonne of fear about losing your buddies, your comrades, about being excluded from the shenanigans and generally ending up as Billy No-Mates.

Honestly, I've found most people are pretty indifferent to it. They shrug and move on. It's not the 70s and you're not a hardboiled journalist who starts lunch at 10.30 with a Martini. Most people just won't care. They care about their car payments, their cholesterol level or their idiot boss and his plan for world domination.

There were people who were a little too interested. Anyone who seems a bit too keen on hearing about your quitting journey is actually saying "HELP!!!". They're just trying to be subtle about it. So be patient, be kind, explain what you feel confident explaining and if all else fails buy them this book.

Having thought quite hard about it, literally for most of the last cup of coffee, I can't remember any occasions that I've come across open hostility. Sure, I've had a lot of blokes taking the mick but it's all good-natured stuff. It's said in the same way that they casually inform me they're sleeping with my wife.

Ultimately, anyone who makes you feel small, anyone who's genuinely cruel, anyone who's out and out hateful is no friend of yours. Ditch them like you ditched Hank.

An ordered mind

What you've probably realised is that below the changes in friendships there was a shift in my thinking. I changed the way I valued relationships. Below the change in my marriage was another change, a seismic shift in priorities. The same was true about the job; I abandoned long held beliefs about what I wanted from gainful employment.

 The order that blossoms externally comes from the order that buds internally.

There are lots of ways of creating more order in your mind. You know this because you're doing it. You've been doing it since you started reading this book, and that reordering is structural. You've changed the way you tramp through the brain forest. You've beaten new neural pathways while letting old ones grow over and disappear.

In fact, you've strengthened the connection between your pre-frontal cortex and your striatum, which is a fancy-pants way of saying you've pumped up your resolve. Your brain is measurably different to how it was before you started reading this. How cool is that? You're a brain surgeon!

Why not keep at it? Start with repeating phrases. You know the power of repetition; you know that your problem was believing the illusion of truth about alcohol. Why did you believe it? You heard it. You became it.

Let's use that power for good.

Real men repeat

You can call repeating phrases whatever you like. Some people would call them mantras; if you don't like that then call them MAN!-tras. All it means is "transport the mind" and that's what you're doing. Transporting your mind from limited, illusionary beliefs to freedom and success. Jump on the mind-bus.

Two phrases I like are "Real Men Quit" and "You're number one!". No surprises there. But here's another. I'm basically a rock star. Every morning as I get out of bed I shout, "Let's rock the day!". Well, most of the time – there are days when even I feel like hitting the snooze button and pretending the world doesn't exist, but 98% of the time that's how I start the day.

It's so simple, why wouldn't you? It makes you want to jump out of bed and kick the morning in the bollocks. A world-changing at-titude starts early. I'm not saying you have to get up at 5am to be a temperance warrior, just start the day like you mean it.

You can come up with your own phrase. It could be as simple as "today is going to be a good day" or something retro like "by the power of Greyskull!"

Obviously, if you want to build this habit then you know what to do. Getting out of bed is the trigger. Shouting "Cocked, locked and ready to rock." is the action. And firing your imaginary sub-machine gun into the air would be a cheeky celebration. So long as it makes you happy it'll create the tracking.

The power of changing your thoughts

Beginning the day well is great. Shouting "You're number one!" with your coffee is great. But there's something deeper going on. What you're doing is changing the way you think about life.

Back in the bad old drinking days I imagine the first thought that crossed your mind as you woke up was probably "oh crap, I'm late", "what did I do last night?" or "is that a sheep?".

Those are some negative thoughts, some bad ways to roll out of bed. Now you're going to start the day with something way more positive. You're taking bits of your life that used to make you unhappy and turning them into little bits of happiness. That's huge. Contrary to popular social media influencers...

 Happiness isn't the big stuff: it's the small moments.

And these changes are easiest in low-pressure situations, like first thing in the morning or when you're making coffee. Of course, if you can learn to do it in these low-stakes environments, then you can hone the skill and start to ramp it up.

Practice makes permanent

Let's remove a few minor annoyances. Pick one thing that lights your fire, the smaller the better, like oat milk. It's not that oat milk annoys me – I'm quite fond of oat milk. It's the cartons I can't stand. My wife seems incapable of putting the empties in the recycling. Annoying, right?

I see a carton that she has considerately put near the recycling – not in it but near it. I have the choice. I could get annoyed and think, "You've placed this carton 67cm from the recycling. 67cm! Not even a metre!! God damn it, go the extra 67cm!!!". Or I could

think something else. For argument's sake let's just stick with "You're number one!".

The carton becomes the trigger. Saying "You're number one!" while I put it in the recycling is my new reaction. The smile is the celebration and we're well on our way to create an attention loop. Actually, we're well on our way to a slice of domestic bliss.

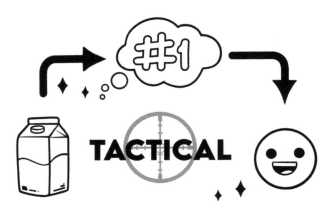

OK, maybe you're thinking that oat milk cartons aren't exactly life changing; it isn't number one problem territory. But think about it. In that moment, when you see that cartoon, it's your number one problem. Spot it. Solve it. Smile.

Get really good at doing it during the easy times and then start doing it during the tough times. Like the Spartans used to say, "sweat more in training, bleed less in battle".

Your personal Battle of Thermopylae

Once you've nailed it with the easy stuff you can start to apply it in more difficult situations. Not necessarily when you're rabidly outnumbered by hordes of angry Persians, just small annoyances where you could improve your day.

I drive a lot. I spend more time than is really healthy on the M25. No disrespect to our friends from the capital, but there are some bloody awful drivers on the London Orbital. I used to swear, shout and generally turn into a rage-ball at the brain-free driving that I was subjected to.

Then it dawned on me. Shouting didn't work. The idiot drivers didn't notice, they drove by, still being a dick. All shouting did was ruin my day.

It has no effect on them, hmm? But it ruins my day, hmm?

Instead of spitting bile at idiotic drivers I decided I'd shout "You're number one!". Admittedly I say it in a passive aggressive way. I'm not perfect.

 Don't try to be Buddha, try to be better.

Now when someone cuts me up or undertakes, I say "You're number one!" with an idiotic grin on my face. Most of the time.

And you know how I do it. Bad driving is the trigger. Saying "You're number one!" is the action. The idiot grin is the celebration. That creates the tracking.

Trigger. Action. Celebration. Tracking. Are we having fun yet?

What I want to stress is that this is just an example. You may not mind overpriced German cars being driven by motor-knobs. But something annoys you. Something ruins your day. And here's the good news – you have the power to change it.

Identify what it is. Work out what you can do differently. Create a celebration. Build Tactical Change. Crash bang! Peace. Happiness. Calm.

And you're ready for it my friend. You've been training your mind like a Spartan trains his spear arm. Man, you're mentally ripped. Go out there and use the advanced stuff. Change your reaction. That's how you change your reality. That's how you change the world.

Every day is today

Fantastic, that's order sorted and you're completely overwhelmed again.

Put the book down. Think about what you have read. Do you have a problem in this area? A number one, burning at the top of the

mountain-type problem? Solve it. Get ready for a new number one problem. Don't forget to celebrate.

No, seriously, take a moment to celebrate. Time is passing and you wouldn't want to miss it.

Some people think you should remember how long you have been sober to the minute. That never appealed to me. I guess I'm not sure why I'd be so aware of how long it was since I haven't done something. It's not like I regularly tell people how long it is since I last shit myself.

I stopped drinking at some point towards the end of May 2015. But I only remember that because it's almost exactly nine months before my daughter was born. They weren't joking about that fertility thing.

Unless you feel inclined to, don't sweat the time and the date but make a mental note of the month and year, maybe try to conceive a child as a handy reminder. Before you know it, a year will pass then two, five, ten. It's worth remembering roughly when you stopped because once a year it'll bring a smile to your face. I like to think of it as my re-birthday. And yeah, I celebrate, you know I still party.

"You can't start a fire. You can't start a fire without a spark.

BRUCE SPRINGSTEEN

"Great to meet you Duncan. Would you like some pizza?"

I smiled. This wasn't the first time I had been offered pizza today. This wasn't the first time I had been offered pizza in the last five minutes.

"No thanks, I'm fine," I replied.

We started to chat about the event. I was trying to get to know people over lunch because I was going to be speaking to them about my new project after it. And they all seemed to be trying to get rid of pizza. The boss had sprung for lunch. In her undying enthusiasm she'd ordered a little too much of the stuff. Boy, were they trying to shift a few slices.

"Hi there, I'm Duncan." It sounded a bit thin-crust. I'd said it too many times.

"Hey Duncan, would you like some pizza," he pointed at the mount of untouched Papa John's boxes.

But this time it was different. This time I heard another voice.

"Ummmmmm, tasty, tasty pizza." I recognised the tone but I couldn't quite place it.

"Look, they've even got the one you like with the olives and the vegan cheese," the silky voice exuded honeyed indulgence.

"Go on, you deserve it, you've worked so hard, have a slice of pizza. Just the one."

"Hank?" I asked.

"Don't worry about me, think about the yummy, yummy pizza."

"Hank, what are you doing here?"

"Never mind that, wouldn't you like a slice of pizza?"

"No, I've already had lunch."

"There's always space for pizza."

"Hank, Hank, Hank," I shook my head, "I think you've forgotten something."

"What?"

"Real men quit!"

"Not pizza as well?"

"I only eat junk food on Friday evening and I think you'll find it's Tuesday lunchtime."

"Is nothing sacred?"

"Quitting is sacred."

"I'm starting to wonder about you."

"Real! Men! Quit!" I started to dance.

"I'm going to go and sit in the corner."

I was awash with a graceful feeling, a kind of glow. A sort of un-formed idea that I could punch holes in the sky, with nothing but the power of my mind.

"So Duncan, what are you talking about today?" said the real, ac-tual person who was really, actually in front of me and in no way an allegorical phantasm that conveniently expressed my internal dialogue.

"Yeah, it's exciting. You see I have this interesting idea…"

REAL MEN FEEL

'm prepared to guess that you don't mind me talking about being strong; real men are strong. You don't have a problem with me talking about creating order; real men have their shit together. You can handle all that. But feeling? Now that's just a bit...

Irrational? Hysterical? Pathetic? Real men don't do emotions.

Really?

What about enjoyment? You can cope with enjoyment, right? You've probably also been surprised, that's non-threatening. You can probably also accept the existence of sadness. What about anger and contempt? You've done those in your time. Disgust is also pretty safe ground.

Then there's fear and you know that it exists, but only in other people...

Congratulations, you've just got to grips with emotions and you didn't have to cry once.

ENJOYMENT

SADNESS

SURPRISE

EMOTIONS
FOR
BEGINNERS

ANGER

CONTEMPT

FEAR

DISGUST

Don't fear the weeper

The basic palette of emotions – enjoyment, surprise, sadness, anger, contempt, disgust and fear – can be mixed together to create more subtle emotions. Add anger to fear and chuck in a dash of contempt, congratulations! You have shame!

> **You have emotions whether you want them or not.**

Let me demonstrate. Imagine that you're walking through the woods and you catch a glimpse of something out of the corner of your eye. In an instant your body floods with adrenaline and you're prepared to either fight the snake or run.

That happens unimaginably quickly because visual information reaches the emotion bit of your brain faster than the vision bit. In other words, your body is feeling the fear before your brain has figured out that it's just a stick.

That happens to everyone with a functioning mind. I don't care how tough you are, unless you have Schmidt for brains, it happens. But it doesn't last forever. The fear only lasts until another part of your brain takes over and redirects things. And there's the truth – you can't stop emotions but you can manage them.

Good news, because you wouldn't want to remove emotions. They colour your life. Think about scoring the winning goal – it wouldn't be the same without a splash of enjoyment, and if it's Oxford United, a chunk of surprise. And when The U's go on to lose the match? If it wasn't for sadness and anger it would be just the same as brushing your teeth. What's life without emotions?

Emotions don't just add chromatic intensity, they make you human. If someone lacks emotions, we call them robotic, and that's the point. Without emotions you may as well be a machine. The bad news is that machines are getting faster, smarter and more ruthless. In fact, you better get to grips with your emotions because they're the only thing you've got to outsmart Skynet.

She comes in colours everywhere

Emotions colour life, but they can also paint it black. They're the down as well as the up. They're at the heart of good mental health and poor mental health.

For the sake of complete transparency, I didn't study anything even vaguely psychiatric at university. What I studied was booze, drugs and a Northern Irish lass who wore too much lipstick. I'm not a substitute for the advice of a mental health professional.

I've also never been diagnosed with any mental health condition, although I've been described as feeble-minded on several occasions. That said, I think it's fair to say that I have what the pros call "lived experience".

You know how stopping drinking stories are supposed to go; you know they have a climactic low point, where rock bottom gets hit in a dramatic and moodily-lit way. Ideally it happens staring into a mirror at four a.m.

That's not what happened to me. My version of rock bottom came when I was waiting at some traffic lights.

All time low

The high street was busy, lots of shoppers, a few scurrying worker bees and more traffic than should really flow through the centre of a town. The kind of slice of life you'd see at midday in any market town with a mediaeval road system.

I was walking back to work after lunch, and by lunch I mean chain-smoking and maybe putting a little brandy in my coffee. But only a little, for flavour.

Things weren't going well. I was stressed due to a big project I was doing outside of work. I was stressed because I had relationship difficulties because I was selfish. Because I was not the lover, friend or partner that my wife deserved.

I was stressed because I was attempting to re-enact the Battle of Bosworth Field with my idiot boss. He was obsessed with minutes. Three minutes late was an affront. It wasn't so much that he felt like I was stealing from him – those 180 seconds were a crime against humanity, to be tried in the International Criminal Court.

On the whole I wasn't in a good state.

I'd begun the miserable trudge back to work. I'd got as far as the inevitable wait for the green man. As I watched the cars crawl past, an eerie silence cloaked the street. There was a moment of solemn stillness. A moment of funereal calm.

Crash.

A wave of emotion broke. I was engulfed in the upsurge. A tsunami of fear and shame and guilt and pain and, over it all, weakness. My chest filled with the unbearable feeling that whatever I did it wouldn't be enough. That whatever I tried, wherever I turned, it would all just crumble. I was about a cigarette paper away from total, irreparable collapse.

I know that it was all going on in my mind. I know that it was only thoughts, just chemical and electrical connections firing in my head, but at that moment it wasn't thought, it was pure feeling. Emotion overtook my body.

It felt like there was a black hole sun in my chest that was straining to get out. Like there was an aching, screaming nothingness that was

REAL MEN QUIT

filling my body, pushing so hard that my ribs were about to breach. A nihilistic void that was dead set on swallowing up my entire life.

I was swamped in a raven dark nightmare but life continued. The shoppers still shopped, the drones still scuttled back to the hive, the cars still pumped out their noxious fumes.

I crossed the road.

I share this for one very simple reason. We all get overwhelmed sometimes. And that's OK. We all get overtaken by our feelings. We all feel the gaping maw trying to break out and consume everything that is good and righteous and light filled. It's normal.

Heck, it's not even surprising. I'd spent the better part of 20 years pouring poison into my body and I'd spent even longer allowing it to stream into my mind. What's surprising isn't that the emotions nearly dragged me down that day, it's that it didn't happen sooner.

Don't bottle it

You've heard of post-traumatic stress disorder (PTSD)? It develops because of exposure to a traumatic event. What gets in the news is soldiers who have developed PTSD during wars, but that trauma could also come from accidents, abuse or any form of violence.

I'm not saying that during your drinking career anything that serious happened to you. If it did then I respectfully suggest now's the time to find some professional help. But what I am saying is that while you were drinking you did many little things that you aren't proud of.

I could write several more books filled with the thousand paper-cut transgressions that made up my drinking career. What happened to you? Maybe you embarrassed yourself. Maybe you threw up into someone's shoes. Maybe you stole. Maybe you lied. Maybe you cheated. Maybe you drove drunk. Maybe you were violent. Maybe you were a victim.

Whatever it was, it's an ocean of emotion – it's trauma. And it's time to move on.

I had all that pain inside, how did I try to move away from it?

I tried to drink it away and I just ended up drowning.

I thought that I'd come up with a great way to get rid of my emotions. I used it every day. I drank some wine; that left me with an empty bottle and I poured my emotions into it. I thought it was a handy receptacle that allowed me to dispose of my emotions in an environmentally-responsible way.

The problem, I now see, is that I wasn't sending my emotions to landfill. I was recycling them, and not in a good way.

I thought I was getting a fresh new bottle every night. But I wasn't. I was pouring my feelings into the same bottle. That bottle just got fuller. My emotions didn't go away when I drank. I bottled them up.

And a lot of us do. We pour them into a little bottle marked 'emotions'. And the bottle is only so big. Eventually, the bottle starts to get full, we keep pouring and hoping, and drinking. And sooner or later it gets too full, and we can't fit any more in.

But we try. We try to pour a little more in and we end up knocking over the bottle. All the feelings come splashing out. Damn it, you split emotions all over the kitchen floor.

I don't know how big your bottle is, but I do know that its capacity is limited. Eventually it gets full. Eventually you needed to actually do something about it's contents. Eventually you have to start to manage your emotions.

Emotions kill

You need to do something because emotions are dangerous. Seriously, a recent study found that repressing your emotions raises your blood pressure. Which means keeping it all inside will break your heart. And not in a weepy, snivelling way, more in a massive heart attack on the toilet, dead like Elvis way.

But maybe The King is not your thing, maybe you don't plan on checking into Heartbreak Hotel. Maybe you only like serious music. Great, just don't end up like Kurt Cobain.

Suicide is too common among men. Men kill themselves at over three times the rate of women and it often stems from unprocessed trauma. Emotions kill.

Don't be afraid of professional help. It's called talking therapy because it involves talking, no thumbscrews, no choke pear, no 24-hour loop of *Frozen 2*. It's not scary. You talk, someone listens and asks the odd question. You get to understand the past, which helps you understand yourself, which helps you succeed. Not scary.

This isn't a book about dealing with trauma, which is a complex subject. If you think you need to do something then do something. Even if you just start with Google – that's the search engine not the dodgy AI therapy bot they're undoubtedly working on.

How did you get here

You don't have to talk to a professional. Talking is therapeutic even if you don't have one of those psychiatrist couches. You could talk to a friend.

But let's face it, as men we're not the best at deep and meaningful chats. Sure, we can name the starting line-up for Oxford's 1986 Milk Cup win, but talking about how we're feeling? Not so much.

You won't be surprised to know that I think at the root of it all is an illusion of truth. Have you ever heard the idea that boys don't cry? Maybe once or twice. Even as little boys we're told to bottle up our emotions rather than express them.

Some relationships also reinforce the danger of expressing emotions. Some women, and by no means all of them, will say that they want a man who cries and talks and thinks and feels but, due to their own relationship trauma, they get upset when their man is anything other than unthinkingly tough.

And let's face it, we don't exactly help ourselves. There are certain environments where even showing concern for another man's wellbeing will be labelled as gay and even the mildest sentiment will elicit a barrage of emasculating jibes. You know the drill: stop whining and man up. You've heard it all before.

And none of that is your fault.

The example your parents set for you, the illusions that they lodged in your head. That's not your fault. They way previous partners have treated you, how they reinforced those beliefs, not your fault. The way your mates treat you, not your fault.

 **It's not your fault that you're like this.
But it is your problem.**

Repeatedly being told to toughen up doesn't toughen you up. It makes you hide your emotions. And that problem's big, like jumpsuit, Vegas Elvis.

Don't bottle it up, because even a Nebuchadnezzar of Champagne can only hold so much. Luckily there's another way. You can carefully pour out small amounts of emotion, a little at a time. That way the bottle won't get full.

It's good to talk

You pour out little bits of emotion by talking – that usually doesn't involve Oxford United winning the League Cup when you were nine. Unless that emotionally scarred you – thanks Ray Houghton. But you know this. Plenty of people have told you that you should talk about your emotions more. But what does that mean?

To start with you need someone who will listen to you. They must be someone trustworthy, but they don't have to be someone you know. You could try a local mental health charity, the Samaritans or Oxford United's 24-hour helpline for the victims of Milk Cup success. What sounds easier to you, talking to a stranger or talking to a friend?

Clearly, they should be able to listen. Sadly, listening is a rare skill. Real listening is about focusing on what someone else is saying, being genuinely interested and not jumping in the moment you think of something even mildly relevant to say.

 Maybe the problem isn't that men don't talk, maybe it's that we don't listen?

Release the pressure

Maybe you're still unconvinced about talking, OK. Think about what you're trying to achieve. You want some safety and connection to another person, then you can express some emotion without fear. What else could provide that?

Journaling might work. I agree it's not for everyone. I can't get on with it. But I also know people who think it's amazing, so try it, it might work. If it does, it'll get a lot of junk out of your head. If it doesn't, you'll end up with a new notebook.

Painting and creative writing can help. Trust me, I got hours of free therapy from writing this book. But to work effectively it has to be your thing. If you think it might be, grab a pencil and scribble.

Clearly journaling, painting and creative writing are solitary pursuits, so be aware they won't necessarily provide the connection. That said, you can find like-minded people in these areas either locally or online.

If you're more physical you could consider dancing, hardcore raving, morris dancing or just turning up the stereo and seeing what happens. Sport could be another good way of sweating out some emotions.

Just to be clear, I don't mean get a punch bag and go ape. Punching your emotions out tends to just make you angry. But if there's a sport you love, which helps you express yourself and creates connections with other people then try it. What's the worst that could happen? You might accidentally improve your mental health while improving your physical health.

I had to go to that place to get to this one

Number one problem or not I am going to strongly suggest you do something right now. Embrace compassion. And start with yourself.

When we look at our lives we're often our hardest critic. We look back on our actions with a level of vitriolic criticism which wouldn't be out of place at the trial of Vladimir Putin.

Do you sometimes respond to your own behaviour in a way that's a bit harsh? Think about it, is what you say to yourself what you would say to a friend in the same position? Probably not. If it was a mate you'd understand, empathise, reassure – you'd show some compassion.

Don't you deserve a bit of benevolent love? God damn it, you do! And you can start right now by changing the way you think about your past. You can do that now because it's really quick.

Doubtless you've done many things that, with hindsight, you wouldn't do again. Things that you're not proud of. Things that make your toes curl just thinking about them. Maybe you did something unforgivable like getting her name wrong while making love. I'm not saying it wasn't wrong to shout your girlfriend's mum's name during sex, but how is the pain serving you?

You can change the way you see those things right now. Instead of seeing them as black marks of pain burnt into what's left of your soul you can see them as marker-posts on a journey.

You are who you are because of what's happened to you. You got to this point, to this moment, because of everything that has happened to you. You couldn't have gotten here without everything that has gone before. If things had been different, you would be different. If you'd travelled a different path you'd be in a different place.

And you've come to a good place. True, it's not exactly where you want to be but today you're closer than you were yesterday and tomorrow you'll be closer still.

There's only one route to here. There's only one way that you could've got to this exact moment. That route was the route you took. You travelled the shattered highway, like so many of your brothers. It wasn't what you wanted but it's led you here. And here's OK. And it's getting better.

Accept that everything you've done, *all* those things, they were just footprints on the broken road. Just steps taking you to this point.

There's no other way to get here than the way you came. That's worth smiling about. The marker-posts are just marker-posts, signs pointing to a better place. Don't feel bad, don't beat yourself up, be compassionate, be human. Forgive, because...

Real men forgive. Yes, they forgive the people who've hurt them but more than that...

 Real men forgive themselves.

Yes, we know...

There now follows the usual warning that's been at the end of the last two chapters. Don't get overwhelmed. Pick your number one problem, solve it, find a new number one problem, solve it.

Great. As far as it goes. But this chapter is different.

There's a strong possibility that you don't want to get to grips with any of what I've just spoken about. There's a strong possibility that you started drinking to distance yourself from your emotions. There's a strong possibility that you've spent years and years actively ignoring your feelings. You've been avoiding them because they're overwhelming, that's the problem.

You probably need to do some emotional heavy lifting, even if you want to shy away from it, even if it seems too scary. Honestly, this is the part of living your best life that isn't easy. It's simple, you have to square up to the stuff you don't want to, but it ain't easy.

On the other hand, you may want to set aside the emotional work because it isn't the most important thing for you at the moment.

Making that call is complicated like the calculus. If you put it on the 'things to tackle later' pile, make sure it's for the right reasons. Don't dodge the difficult stuff. Real men don't just arm-wrestle, they tussle with the tough questions too.

Whatever you decide to do, however you decide to move forward, remember the old maxim, "talk is cheap." It really is. So try talking about what bothers you with a friend. It's easier than you think and it's cheap. All you have to do is buy them a coffee.

Trust me, unburdening yourself is liberating. It's like ending a hard day by stripping down to your pants and watching a western.

" Here's a little song I wrote, you might want to sing it note for note.

BOBBY McFERRIN

The barman put a small apple juice on the bar and a large charge on my debit card. I swung my head round searching for a friendly face.

The pub was full. Everyone was laughing, joking and enjoying general purpose fun. Apart from me. I didn't feel like I was about to enjoy a pleasant afternoon with a few friends. I felt like I was about to explain to a room full of five-year-olds why I enjoy punching kittens.

I sank my drink like my throat was on fire.

It was possible that I might be a little bit nervous. Should I man up and try to find the guys or should I cut my losses and run out of the pub screaming?

I thought back to the glory days. Once upon a time an empty glass would have led to a full glass.

Apparently drinking was not drinking when it was apple juice. Now you come to mention it, I was starting to wonder if there was a difference between morris dancing and morris dancing while drinking. Actually, I was starting to worry that I might not be able to do it sober. Would my legs dance without a lubrication of cider?

I took a breath and reminded myself that I'd only stopped drinking, I hadn't stopped living. I definitely hadn't stopped showing off and wearing silly hats. I could enjoy today, even if I was going to spend it surrounded by drinkers drinking drinks in drinking dens.

As if by magic Dave appeared, a little sparkle in his eye reminding me that he was endowed with more than a slice of cheeky chap.

"Wanna beer?" he asked.

Simple question: easy answer. Yet it stood there like a monolith. A huge weight raised to its apex by incredible motive force, hanging for a second and then falling, inevitable. A Delphic vision that crumpled into my mind with the shock of what I could become.

The knowledge that this question was a turning point, a fork on the road. Saying yes was just following a path, but where did that trail lead? What would that track turn me into?

It wouldn't turn me into Dave, a slightly out of shape dancer who willed the alcohol out of his glass with an over efficient throat.

No, I'd become something much worse. Something darker. Something glacial. Something lost. Summer's youth wilted in a frozen prison.

I shuddered.

"A glass of water," I squeaked, "please."

It took a moment to register.

"Water?"

"Water."

"Really?"

"Really."

"Suit yourself." He pushed into the queue for the bar.

*

Water in hand, I made my way outside to see who else was here. The beer garden resembles an explosion in a haberdashers: lots of ribbons, lots of bells and fake florists' worth of counterfeit flowers.

"Hey Duncan, do you want a beer?" asked Dave. Not the same one, this was a different Dave.

"Real Men Quit" shouted my head.

"No thanks, Dave, I'm all right with water." my mouth said out loud.

I pushed further into the group with an increasing sense of pleasure. The earlier anxiety was receding like winter gives way to spring. I realised I shared more with these people than just a beer. We shared a tradition, a passion, an unquenchable need to put flowers all around our hats.

"Afternoon Duncan, do you want a beer?" asked Dave. Yeah, there really were that many blokes called Dave in my morris side.

"Real men quit." I mouthed in silent prayer.

"No thanks, Dave."

"Really?" the answer stopped him in his tracks.

"Yeah, I quit."

"Oh... err that's... err yeah..." he looked like he wanted to say more but he was conflicted.

"It's cool, Dave, get a drink and we can talk about it later."

"Yeah... err sure." He walked off, a little dazed and confused.

Needless to say, I was smiling. What a great day to dance. What a great day to live, maybe a great day to share the joy?

REAL MEN UNDERSTAND

What's the basis of understanding? Understanding the world is important but self-awareness is where it's at. What's the basis of self-awareness? Understanding the difference between what you *want* and *what* you actually *need*.

Let's consider Han Solo. What does he want? Money, lots of money. He's motivated by nothing more than cold hard cash. That's why he ended up in the wrong crowd stealing starship fuel. Money, that's what he wants.

But what does he need? He needs to belong. He needs friends. He needs to be able to see himself as a good person, the kind of person who does the right thing, who's on the right side, who helps the people he loves.

That's why he comes back. He gets the money after he's transported Luke and Leia to the rebel base. They pay him, he smiles, he leaves. He has got exactly what he wants.

But he's not satisfied, because he hasn't got what he needs. He hasn't got the sense of belonging, the friends, the identity. He hasn't got the love. So he comes back, saves his friends, kicks some ass, gets a medal and sleeps well at night because he has got not what he wants but what he needs.

The new hope is not the rebellion, or the destruction of the death star or even the return of the Jedi.

 The new hope is self-awareness.

Solo-awareness

Maybe self-awareness sounds like a strange concept. Maybe you're thinking how can I not know myself? I mean, I've known myself for years.

These days I look back on all the time I spent drinking and I can see it for what it was. I was chasing what I wanted, not what I needed. And that went double for that girl from Bratislava – I wanted her, oh how I wanted her. But it turned out that she was an atrocious person hiding behind an amazing ass. I wanted the hard bottom, but I sure as heck didn't need the hard-ass attitude.

I wanted to party, I wanted pleasure, I wanted to escape, I wanted oblivion.

What I needed was peace and calm, love and understanding, energy and focus. I found that by quitting. That's what helped me support my family, strengthen my friendships, build my fitness and develop my fortune. Those are the things that allowed me to create the platform on which I could do good honest work, the kind of work that matters.

It's taken a while to understand my upbringing, to understand the world I live in, to understand who I am. In short, to figure out the difference between what the world thinks I should do, what I want to do and what I *need* to do.

It's a journey you've been on too. Remember how, when you stopped drinking, you used understanding. You didn't use strength. You understood the illusion of truth that the world has tried to flood your brain with. You understood the world better but, crucially, you have begun to understand yourself.

Find yourself, man

To get where you need to go you'll have to delve pretty deep. Let's get it out of the way right now: who are you? It's a toughie, but the real question is who do you need to be?

The question isn't about your job, it isn't about your relationship, it definitely isn't about the 'which Jedi are you?' quiz on Facebook. When the bucket hits the bottom of the well, who do you need to become?

Tough question. So tough it's special forces sniper stuff; I'm asking you to hit a target moving in one direction from a helicopter flying in the other. What you need to be will change over time. Today's answer won't necessarily hit the bullseye tomorrow.

We could look at it by asking other questions: what matters to you? What gives your life meaning? What's important to you? What makes you excited? What can only you offer the world? Luke, what's your destiny? At this point you probably expect me to launch into a questionnaire.

Thankfully, this isn't that kind of book. Stuff like that can be helpful, but you're probably already fed up with questions. And you aren't going to find yourself by doing a quiz. You won't find the subtle line that divides what you want from what you need in a multiple choice.

Finding my voice

Way back when I thought black rollneck jumpers were cool, Marlboro was a positive lifestyle choice and being a writer would get me laid, I appeared as Konstantin in Chekov's stage play *The Seagull*. Konstantin is an angsty, self-obsessed man-boy who labours under the delusion that he's a great writer. I was basically typecast. The director even said I had the right hair.

We did the show. Afterwards I started to forget my lines, but one phrase stuck with me, "I have difficulty finding my voice."

That line obsessed me for years. I spent much of the first decade that I struggled to become a writer – and get laid – trying to find my

voice. I discussed it with friends, did self-evaluation tests and spent a good deal of time navel-gazing. I never found my voice.

Actually, I did. But not by doing any of that. My voice just sort of snuck up on me. After working solidly for years, after producing a good deal of rubbish, I found my voice. There it was, shouting out from a dubious messianic zombie film I scribbled one hazy weekend.

The point is that I found my voice as a writer by writing. No one is born fully formed. Literally no one ever pops out of the womb with a clear understanding of the difference between what they want and what they need.

 You find out who you are by living.

I wrote, I failed, I wrote some more, I developed an aesthetic philosophy and I devoted myself to it.

There's only one way to find your place in life. Strive. Fail. Create. Live. Then double down. Han Solo didn't fill out a self-development exercise to work out that he should go back to the Death Star. Han solved big fat number one problems.

Yeah, but how?

If that sounds a little vague then let's go all science guy on the problem. Let's design an experiment. Which won't be dull, because the experiment is your life. Think of living as a problem to be solved. Don't jump to conclusions. Work through the process and find the best course of action. Heck, you can blow up the chemistry block if that's what it takes.

Think about one action or habit that you either want to start or stop or change or improve. Then follow this study design: What am I doing? Why am I doing it? Should I continue? Form a plan. Test the plan. Repeat as desired.

Don't forget the safety glasses

Let's consider real life questions like should I borrow money from Jabba the Hutt or should I be drinking this much coffee? I've never met any slug-like crime lords, but I do drink a fair amount of coffee so let's go with the java dependence.

WHAT AM I DOING?

You should arrive at granular, specific answers. In that spirit, I drink approximately 1.857 cups of coffee a day, and it's strong coffee too. I spend around £30 a week on it.

WHY DO I DO IT?

This time we're looking for honesty. My slightly defensive response would be "it helps me write". And obviously coffee can help with energy and focus. I also use it as a way of renting space on a table in a fine coffeehouse. It's noisy but I like that; I don't like working alone or in silence, probably because I'm deeply insecure.

SHOULD I CONTINUE?

OK, OK, I don't sleep as well when I drink coffee. I know this because when I don't drink coffee I sleep better. But I think there's some credibility to the argument that it helps me work.

PLAN

An experiment. I should keep everything else the same and drink mint tea instead for two weeks.

TEST

Having measured my output and my sleep from two weeks of coffee drinking, I should compare the results of two weeks of mint tea drinking.

Now that's what I call science. I'm like the reincarnation of Francis bloody Bacon. If you can apply that level of scrutiny to even one slice of your life, then you will massively increase your self-awareness.

You know it works

The basis of what I've just described is what you've been learning to do throughout this book. It must have dawned on you that I have ulterior motives, and I do. I don't just want you to learn a system that'll allow you to control your drinking, I want you to internalise it so you can use it to control your life. I want you to have the freeman's freedom.

That and I've been dropping subliminal hints that you should purchase additional copies of this book. Come to think of it, your Uncle Geoff should read it; he's drunk so much that his life has turned to custard.

Think deeper. What have you been up to while wading your way through all these badly wrought metaphors and cheaply purchased gags?

You've looked at your life objectively. Yes, the focus has been alcohol but as alcohol became so tightly bound up with everything you do, you've actually taken a pretty decent look at your whole life.

But more than that you've engaged the bit of your brain that accurately does the thinking. You've taken the part of your mind, what we call John Connor, and you've used him to reprogramme your inner Terminator. That relentless force in your head that does stuff on autopilot. In short, you've been thinking about your thinking. You become some sort of mind-wielding thought-ninja.

You've asked yourself: What am I doing? Why am I doing it? Should I continue? Then you made a plan. Now you're testing it.

That plan revolved around our three friends, trigger, action and celebration, but it's still a plan. By implementing that plan you have harnessed the power of your mind to drive that change.

Amazing stuff. Sure, you solved your problem with alcohol. Sure, you've learnt how to solve other problems while you did it, which is stupendous. But, and here's the real kicker, you've learned a huge amount about yourself.

More precious than the ability to live a sober life, more precious than the ability to solve problems, is the ability to know yourself well enough to work out *which* problems you need to solve. To work out what matters to you, what gives your life meaning, what your destiny is. To figure out what your number one problem is and then solve the shit out of it.

You've grasped that ethereal difference between need and want. But, most important of all, you've started to work out who the hell you need to be.

Life is on the streets

Go out there with a grin on your face because you have the skills and drills to solve all your problems, and the wisdom to work out what your number one problem is. Solve. Repeat. Ditch the money. Destroy the Death Star. Get the medal. Grin.

I don't need to give you the usual warning about not getting overwhelmed because now you have the self-awareness not to. Instead I'm going to ask you to be gentle on yourself. Seriously, be kind to yourself: get yourself something nice for dinner, watch a film, you can even go back to bed if you want.

Remember that you're not the Han Solo that has just got the medal after saving the day. You're also not the Han that was running scams on the streets of Corellia at the age of ten. But you're probably closer to the start of that journey than the end.

Remember that Han became the Han by flying ships, taking risks and learning to love the Wookiee. He did it by travelling the galaxy and shaking it down. He did it by breaking his heart and banging his head.

And if that sounds like hard work, it's because it *is* hard work. But it's honest work – well, sort of. The kind of work that helps you sleep well at night even if you do drink too much coffee.

Take a moment to chill, and once you're rested go out and hit the galaxy like a rhino that's just been bitten on the bum.

One request

I don't know what you're supposed to be doing with your time on this earth. But I'd love to hear your success story. Message me and we'll celebrate your success together.

I hope I've managed to resist the temptation to just tell you what to do over the preceding pages. But there is one thing that I'm going to ask you to do. No obligations but if you're feeling generous...

Look out for your brothers. About 8 million men are drinking more than they should and that's only in the UK. Not all of them will accept that they have a problem. Some will try to tough it out, some will laugh it off, some will be so desperate to change the subject that they'll start talking about *Strictly Come Dancing*. They all depend on alcohol for something. And there's the problem.

They need help.

They need *your* help. Support them, offer them non-threatening advice, help them however you can. And you could even – subtle hint – buy them a copy of this book.

More than anything else, stand in your truth. Be a real man. Show them that there is a different way. You never achieve much by pushing people somewhere they don't want to go. But if you can show them how great where you're standing is then they'll come in their droves.

Live the life everyone deserves to live. And live out loud.

REAL MEN REALLY SMASH IT

W hat makes a real man? I've struggled with that question over the last couple of years and I've come to a conclusion. I can't tell you. Sorry.

But that's precisely what makes it exciting. There are as many legitimate definitions of real manhood as there are real men. Masculinity is flexibility. You are flexibility.

 You can be anything. And that's exciting.

The possibilities are literally endless. You can be whatever you need to be. Never forget that you are enough but you won't find yourself by looking inside. Even Gandhi knew that, and boy was he keen on meditating. You find yourself by living and working.

And yes, you can have a day off every now and again. I'm not pushing the hustle, grind, 'sleep when you're dead' schtick. Remember, we solve and we don't get overwhelmed.

Take time for yourself. Non-productive time helps you discover new and interesting things. I've recently been through a profound and transcendent inner transformation that involved falling off my inline skates. Apparently, I'm the kind of guy who's proud of having cuts and scrapes on his elbows, who knew?

Keep on keepin' on

As we come to the end of our time together, I'm genuinely excited about what you're going to do. You have so much potential inside you; it's been waiting to break out for years and now you're free of the poison it's going to start to flow like the mighty Zambezi.

Please, please, please let me know. I want to celebrate your triumphs too. I want to meet the real man that you're becoming. Email me, find me on the socials or come round my house and play One Direction on my lawn. Let's party!

The last thing I want to do is put a downer on things. But I'm going to because I want to give you a final warning.

What I'm asking you to do is hard. It's hard because it'll take work and work is effort. You'll have to fight against the urge to sit on the sofa and watching Netflix. Don't get me wrong, there's nothing wrong with sitting on the sofa and watching Netflix; I do it. What I mean is don't do it like it's a full-time job.

You have to avoid the path of least resistance – the path of comfy chairs and comfy telly. But you also have to avoid the path of not quite the least resistance. In some ways this is even worse. This is the path where you do things; you keep busy and you get proud because you're doing stuff. But what you're doing is easy. You're doing what you want to, *not* what you need to. You're solving your number twenty-seven problem.

You're Han Solo chasing the money. Outrunning Imperial blockades is easy when you have a ship like the Millennium Falcon. Come on Han, remember the friendship, the identity, the love. Those involve hard choices and difficult action, but they're more rewarding than cold hard coaxium cash.

Darth Robbins

Imagine that you go to the gym a lot. You make your body strong, but you neglect your heart and you neglect your spirit. You end up with iron pectorals, but you still lack feeling, you still lack understanding. Are you solving problems?

It's a little-known fact that Darth Vader regularly attended Tony Robbins's seminars. He was a self-development nut. He had a shelf full of motivational books, a vision board and a rock-solid plan about how he was going to be the best evil overlord in history. Stalin, Hitler, Putin, they'd have nothing on him. Was he solving problems? Sure.

Was he solving the right problems?

Look, there's nothing wrong with working on your strength. Just don't work *only* on your strength because you'll end up like Vader, Hitler and Putin: a megalomaniac cockwomble. The force needs balance. Strength and order need feeling and understanding.

Never forget

Never, ever, ever forget how bad drinking was. Part of you may be thinking, "what are you talking about Duncan? I'd never do that". Trust me, people do. And it's not really their fault. Their brains are to blame.

Yes, I have one more fancy-pants psychological theory for you before you go. I think it'll help. It's called fading affect bias, but you can call it FAB, particularly if you remember *The Thunderbirds*, and I mean the clacky-mouthed, visible wires version.

It's a pretty simple idea – like all the best psychology your grandma could have thought of it. Fading affect bias is our tendency to exaggerate the good and forget the bad.

You can see it every time you look back on your childhood. You tend to forget about boring things, the times your legs hurt because you had to walk or how much you had to tidy your room – you minimise the negative. What you remember are those endless summer days, the pure joy of getting covered in mud and that Action Man jeep that you wanted for years and finally got one birthday – you maximise the positive. Oh, that jeep.

It makes sense. The bad bits are bad, and the good bits are good. If your mind worked the other way round, you'd be depressed the whole time. If our ancestors hadn't had FAB working for them, they'd have spent their lives sitting in their cave wailing about how hard it was to find bushes with berries, rather than thinking about those tasty, tasty berries.

Which was all well and good 15,000 years ago when the good bits were truly good. But now it doesn't serve you so well. Now we remember the illusion of truth and think that it was good. Our minds sneakily forgets all the pain and suffering that alcohol caused and just starts to fantasise about a cold beer on a warm day with a hot woman.

Stop it, brain!

Actually, don't stop it. By all means fantasise about the hot woman. It was always about her anyway, the beer added nothing but dehydration, blurring, reduced joy, vomit and a limp dick.

 Remember the reality, not the illusion.

Be aware that your brain is going to go all FAB on you. FAB is just Hank, just a badly programmed Terminator, just the illusion of truth. It's trying to fool you. Engage the bit of your mind that can think; remember that alcohol always took more than it gave. And the reason the hot woman liked you wasn't the cold beer; it was because you're a real man.

Make sure that all the illusionary positives of drinking are gone. Then there's nothing for FAB to seize upon.

Rocking this party eight days a week

Throughout this book I've been going on about how much I like to party. You may have guessed that when I say party I don't mean the no sleep till Brooklyn, waking up before I get to sleep type of party. Those days are gone and, frankly, good riddance to them.

Maybe there's still a little part of you that yearns for the glory days, a bit that thinks any blowout that you can get done and still be in bed at 10.30 doesn't count. I get that.

But in the name of Mike D and everything that is most ill, please, you gotta fight for your right to party.

Partying is important. Celebrating is important. Dancing your arse off in the grips of rhythmic madness is important. Don't lose the passion. Don't lose the thrill. Don't lose the buzz. Get intoxicated by life.

Because if you enjoy not drinking then you won't drink. If you hate alcohol-free living you'll quit quitting and end up drinking Brass Monkey on the corner with people who have more STDs than teeth.

Fight for your right to party. And remember, when they complain about the noise, aw, they're just jealous it's the Beastie Boys.

Be what they need

You should serve the people you love. That'll make the world a better place. Heck, if you can serve the people you don't love you'll probably even usher in a utopian dreamland. Just serve. Be what they need you to be. When they need strength, be strong. When they need order, be ordered. When they need feelings, feel. When they need understanding, understand.

And, once you've done it, spend some time falling off your skates, watching Star Wars, drinking mint tea or whatever milks your goat.

The great news is you can do it. You can be Luke if that's what they need. You can be Han if that's what they need. Heck, if they need it, you can even be an Ewok. Just don't be Jar Jar Binks because he's a floppy-eared penis-burger.

Go out there and live. Keep an eye out for the hugenormous number one problems. Solve 'em. Smile. That's how you find meaning. That's how you find yourself, not in a self-help course run by the latest self-proclaimed guru, but in life.

Find yourself by living. By serving the people you love. By being what the world needs you to be. By tempering your strength with order, feeling and understanding. By stepping into your power no matter how frightening it might be. By having a laugh while you're doing it. And by inviting me round for a party afterwards.

You will find the way because you are the way. Hold your head up high and never forget…

 **Real Men Quit**

" Oh, I've been smilin' lately. Dreamin' about the world as one and I believe it could be. Someday it's going to come.

Cat Stevens

The sun was shining through the coffee cup steam. The vapour twisted and swirled in the shaft of honeyed light like a world class figure skater executing a dizzying spin. I gently lifted it to my lips. That first bitter-smooth wave of caffeinated bliss coated my mouth.

"You're number one!" I bellowed as I leapt onto the coffee table and began to shake what my mother gave me.

Well, I didn't actually start to dance. In my head, I was dancing. In my head, the audience was chanting my name. In my head, they were throwing their lacey knickers.

I pushed further back into the sofa and grinned. I was content. Not smugly so, because life was not perfect, but comfortably satisfied. Just safe in the knowledge that right here, right now, it's alright.

"Please don't take my sunshine away," drifted into my consciousness thanks to some tinny Bluetooth speakers on the other side of the cafe.

Jon would have approved. It's the marching tune of our old college militia. The sound system, on the other hand... let's just say he would have described it as a frog farting in an elevator. I smiled. I miss him. I always will.

I wish I could have shared with him what I know now. That thought brings me a sharp stab of regret, pain, shame. I can't share it, and even if I could he wouldn't have listened. Heck, back in the day I wouldn't have listened. The lad I was then would have dismissed the man I am now with a casual flick of the wrist.

I wish it was different. With all my heart and the ragtag remnants of my soul I yearn for it to be different, but it is not. Jon is gone.

He was a way-marker on the journey. A huge, scruffy, hilarious, beautiful, terrible, kind, misunderstood, loved and contrary meander on a broken road.

I cannot go back. I cannot change what happened.

I will never give up the sorrow. I wouldn't want to even if I could. But I will also never give up the joy. He still makes me laugh, still brings me happiness and I have no doubt he still looks down and wonders why the hell I chop garlic that way.

Maybe one day we'll meet again. Maybe one day I'll be able to explain that he was enough. That he never needed the booze. That the whole universe was inside him just wanting to burst out. Maybe I could help him see the potential we all saw.

I consider this for a moment. Maybe it's not him that needs to understand? Maybe I should take my own advice?

Maybe I will, because the man who sits here today is very different from the one Jon knew.

I look up and smile at a familiar face coming towards me. He started out as a friend of Jon's, but now I'm proud call him a friend of mine.

It's been a while; kind of a lot has happened since I last saw his face. It breaks into a grin. It has changed and changed and changed but it is more or less the same.

He greets me like it's been a handful of days rather than a fistful of years. The reunion is temporarily halted by his desire to grab a coffee.

In the pause I realised I should take my own advice. I should let the universe flow out of me because it's the people that are here and *now that matter. They're the ones that need. They're the ones that hunger for rest.*

They're the ones that I must help; show them that ease comes not from finding yourself but from searching. Gratitude comes not from reaching the destination but from moving forward.

Because life is movement. The trick is to look up every now and again and enjoy the view.

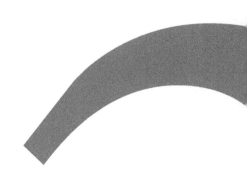

SECTION

Get With the Brogramme

And a Bit

Over the last few hundred pages you've probably noticed that I like a question. Thus, it will probably not come as a big surprise that I've got an entire quiz for you.

What's your sober style?

Have you ever wondered if you're 'The Brain' or 'The Friend', 'The Dynamo' or 'The Reflector? Almost certainly not, but you must have noticed that there's too many opinions on the internet. If you want to work out what advice to take then you need to know your sober style.

Your sober style will help you cut through the forest of guidance like an average footballer cuts through Oxford United's defence.

The sober styles were born on my podcast, Flatpack Sober. I've interviewed quite a few people who've got good at sober but I realised that, while they have many similarities, they weren't all doing the same things. I wondered why.

So I started asking them too many questions about how they assemble flatpack furniture. And whether they like IKEA meatballs (no one does, they lie). And that's how I figured out the four sober styles. Thus the quiz got built – despite the baffling instructions and spare screws.

Hack your way through all the internet dross by learning your sober style. It's about four minutes and twenty three clicks away. It'll help you figure out what's right for you.

Just visit: https://flatpacksober.com/

Are you ready to step up as a sober warrior?

You want to join the sober army? You want to break the alcohol industry and then really get started on changing the world? Great, I'm here to help.

My programmes work.

They work because they're based on an assumption. I assume that you're actually pretty good at what you do. That you are successful and, dare I say it, high functioning.

It was alcohol that brought you down.

And you're pleased you've ditched it but there's a metric crap tonne of other things that you need to do to get where you want to get. You're starting to worry that all that other stuff is going to stop you kicking ass and taking names.

Be cool, I got you.

I'll walk down the road with you

I'm here to keep you company on what can be a difficult journey. There are three pillars to my technique: Science, Experience, Humour

SCIENCE

I trained with the world's most successful stop smoking service, studied at Cornell University, the Chartered Management Institute and a windowless room in Peterborough; I've read a ton of books and interviewed a bunch of experts, and I did it all for one reason.

So you don't have to.

I've understood the science for you. You can sit back, safe in the knowledge that what I say is based on proper, white-coat research done by dead clever people. But best of all, I'll explain it to you in terms you understand. I promise I will never use the phrase "Neuron hyperpolarization".

Useful stuff. In language you can understand.

EXPERIENCE

I've been there, I've done that, I've got the T-shirt. I'm not wearing it because it has kebab stains on it, but I really do have it.

If you've paid any attention to the last hundred-odd pages you'll know that I was drinking too much and pretending that pizza was some sort of snack. Worst of all, I was desperately trying to run away from my problems. But I wasn't running away from anything, I was really storing up those problems for a future tsunami of shit.

Trust me, we ain't so different.

HUMOUR

What is life without a bit of fun? You want to stop drinking; you don't want to stop living so I promise you my sessions won't be dull. They get serious, they get heavy, but I always try to crowbar in at least one nob gag.

Because, after all, what's the point in being alive if you can't have a laugh at genitalia?

Because I only have limited seats available on the coaching programme, I am super choosy about who I work with.

It's not that I don't want to help everyone. I kinda do, but I only have 24 hours a day. So I only work with the rebels, the creatives, the bringers of joy, the iconoclasts, the kind of people who see the world and think "wow, that's lame, we can do so much better than that".

Good job brother. But before you go out and change the world you might need to do a bit of work on yourself.

Apply for the programme here: https://www.bhaskaranbrown.com/the-sober-warrior-programme/

Like the soundtrack?

Of course you do, you still rock. Get the Spotify playlist here: https://www.bhaskaranbrown.com/tunes/

WHY IS THERE ONLY ONE NAME ON THE COVER?

O K, so I drank most of the coffee but I certainly didn't put this book together alone.

There are many people that I need to thank, this is going to get long quickly. Which means I need to just chuck people into general thank you buckets, which is neither classy nor gracious but I'd like the acknowledgements not be the longest chapter.

THE PEOPLE THAT MAKE MY LIFE WORK.

Leela, Sreeja, Grandma and Grampy, Laura-Jane Baxter, John Hayns, Deborah Henley and the amazing Kristel Parayo.

THE REAL CREATIVE PEOPLE

Tanja Prokop (cover design), Martin Wackenier (photography), Graciela Aničić (interior design), Iulian Thomas (illustrations), Robin Triggs (line edit) and Tommy Crabtree (development edit).

SOME EXPERTS WHOSE IDEAS I PINCHED

Cris Hay, The Alex J Williams, Sam Bishop, George Anderson, Lynda Shaw PhD, Edd Rayner, R. Michael Anderson and Anthony Stears.

THE FREE STREET BAND

Faris Aranki, Oli Hudson, Matt Parker, Tim Patmore, Alan Hayes, Daniel Dzikowski, Andrew Fraser, Raedmund Jennings, James Ainsworth, Rob Charlton, Harley O'Donoghue, Mike Pagan, Katharine Purser, Toby Rivas and many others that I've probably neglected. Sorry.

THE SOBER WARRIORS

I'd also like to thank everyone I've ever coached, I can't name them because many of them are now running AF special ops but they all elevated my thinking in one way or another.

THE CAFFEINE NATION

Nothing gets done without the ongoing love and support that I get from the good people of RnR, Abingdon. It's their coffee that makes me shout.

FINALLY...

And a big thank you to you for reading this. Without you it's all just ego.

Milton Keynes UK
Ingram Content Group UK Ltd.
UKHW020614241023
431227UK00006B/217